GRACE
NOTES

ALEXANDRA STODDARD

GRACE NOTES

AVON BOOKS ◆ NEW YORK

AVON BOOKS
A division of
The Hearst Corporation
1350 Avenue of the Americas
New York, New York 10019

Copyright © 1993 by Alexandra Stoddard
Grace Notes™ are a registered trademark of Alexandra Stoddard, Inc.
Illustrations by Stephen Freeburg
Published by arrangement with the author
ISBN: 0-380-72197-X

Published in hardcover by William Morrow and Company, Inc.; for information address Permissions Department, William Morrow and Company, Inc., 1350 Avenue of the Americas, New York, New York 10019.

First Avon Books Trade Printing: November 1994

AVON TRADEMARK REG. U.S. PAT. OFF. AND IN OTHER COUNTRIES, MARCA REGISTRADA, HECHO EN U.S.A.

Printed in U.S.A.

OPM 10 9 8 7 6 5 4 3 2 1

To my godmother, Mitzi Christian, who gave me
a bluebird of happiness pin when I was a
little girl and who actively nurtured
my quest, always with
grace and love

"**W**rite it in your heart that every day is the best day in the year. No man has learned anything rightly, until he knows that every day is Doomsday....We owe to genius always the same debt, of lifting the curtain from the common, and showing us that divinities are sitting disguised.... In daily life, what distinguishes the master is the using those materials he has, instead of looking about for what are more renowned, or what others have used well....In stripping time of its illusions, in seeking to find what is the heart of the day, we come to the quality of the moment....It is the depth at which we live, and not at all the surface extension, that imports.

"Then it flows from character, that sublime health which values one moment as another, and makes us great in all conditions, and is the only definition we have of freedom and power."

Ralph Waldo Emerson

FOREWORD

Since I can remember, I've enjoyed writing down thoughts, ideas, inspirations and practical tips I wanted to remember and put to use in my daily life. These became my grace notes. Whenever I read something, heard something, saw something, felt something or figured out something that rang a bell inside me, I wrote it down. I used little spiral notebooks or pads, anything handy.

But it wasn't until I found myself in a wonderful paper-supply store in Paris in the sixties — you may not know it, but the French take their paper stores seriously — that I discovered the ideal vehicle for recording and preserving my grace notes. I inherited a love for beautiful paper from my mother but over the last few decades I've let this enthusiasm become something approaching an obsession (recorded in detail in *Gift of a Letter*). That mild spring day in Paris I went from the Right Bank to the Left Bank in search of four-by-six index cards. The smooth one-hundred-pound paper invited a fountain pen to glide across its surface. I could color-code my notes in pale pink, green, yellow and blue. Even the white cards had a grid of half-centimeter squares in pale lilac or blue. I became addicted to this geometric design that spares me from facing a blank surface.

I went on a binge. I bought up the French file cards in every store I could find. Paper is heavy. Every so often I had to stop at a café, sip *café au lait*, relax, dream up a few grace notes and then continue on my hunt. Nothing but a closed door stopped me from walking in. I was compulsive.

A few years ago I read somewhere that the author of *Lolita*, Vladimir Nabokov, though flexible about his writing schedule, was insistent on using lined bristol cards. While spiral notebooks are what I use to write my books, these cards are ideal for random thoughts.

During that Paris trip, the seeds of another idea began germinating. Since my days as an art student I've enjoyed going to museums and buying postcards of paintings and sculpture that I have been struck by. This habit has resulted in an accidental collection. This casual, spontaneous act evolved into the idea for a book, *The Postcard as Art*, in which I reproduced many of the postcards I'd enjoyed selecting over the years. Ever since childhood I've loved sending cards to friends with a little scribbled grace note — a word of encouragement, a quote, a thought, an insight, a question.

Postcards and my French file cards are of the same size and I have been storing both in shoe boxes, which I have found both comforting and practical. Eventually I had a carpenter build cubbies in my home to store these labeled boxes, floor to ceiling, catalogued by artist, author, and idea. These treasured shoe boxes hold great sources of inspiration for me, and, of course, they are a rich mine of useful references for books and lectures.

Readers often ask me which one of my books I like best and which one was the most fun to write. Invariably it is the one I'm writing. I love the intensity of this mysterious creative process — I look forward to the challenges, the stimulation and the illumination. In Dr. Samuel Johnson's apt words: "The process is the reality." I too am process-oriented. I love the doing, the work. I enjoy abandoning myself to the project, not knowing how it will all turn out.

I have come to understand that there are no beginnings, that everything is interconnected, and I don't like endings. While I enjoy seeking meaning in the unknown, I am particularly exhilarated by the ever-deepening journey of discovery and exploration.

The search for truth and beauty has been going on since the beginning of civilization. As we approach the twenty-first century, we reflect on what has already been expressed that may bring light, truth and life to our own experiences. Whatever has been said before can acquire new meaning through the unique filter of our own character, beliefs, values and consciousness. Wisdom is ageless and timeless — a reminder that human nature hasn't changed much since the Stone Age. We have always needed to eat, sleep and bathe, but how we perform these daily functions defines us uniquely. How we think and feel, what attitudes we develop, reveal our values and character.

In the early eighties, over a lunch meeting with my literary agent and friend Carl Brandt, I discussed my desire to incorporate these random thoughts at the end of each chapter in the book I was planning. "Ah, Grace Notes," said the wise Carl. Years later, in 1986, this book came out under the title *Living a Beautiful Life*, and my grace notes were published for the first time.

We reflect on our lives, drawing from the wisdom of the past and thinking about our hopes for the future. R.W.B. Lewis, in his Foreword to Cynthia Griffin Wolff's biography of Emily Dickinson, tells us, "The story of modern literature bears recurring witness to the conversion of loss into gain, to radical deprivation leading to great creative accomplishment."

As we try to envisage what the world will be like for our grandchildren and imagine who will inherit the good and bad we leave behind, we pause to think of those who have shaped our attitudes. We pay homage to those spirits who have expanded our potential for understanding the unique circumstances of our lives and who have given us hope and courage to be strong and live bravely. We will always be fascinated by the thoughts of others, and by the way they have expressed their truths and insights, because they are the real teachers. They have shared with us the truth as they have experienced it.

In 1959, my aunt, Ruth Elizabeth Johns, an international social worker, decided to take her three oldest nieces around the world. The summer before our odyssey she sent two cartons of books to New

Hampshire where I was working as a camp counselor and tennis coach. I was sixteen, and I found her assignment daunting. The first book I picked up was *The Wisdom of Confucius*, by someone born in 551 B.C.! I had to put down *The Great Gatsby* I was avidly reading and pay attention. It dawned on me she didn't want to waste her hard-earned money in taking around the world an undereducated design student who didn't have a clue the world extended beyond Europe.

God bless her! Aunt Betty dumped a big load on me that July — fifty-four books, to be precise, and we were leaving in less than four months. That first evening, clutching Confucius, down at the counselors' cabin by the lake, I watched the sun set listening to taps, the nightly bugle rippling across the water:

> "Day is done, gone the sun,
> from the hills, from the lakes,
> from the sky… safely rest…
> day is done."

That still Saturday evening, I began to read this strange tome about Eastern culture. In the days that followed, I picked up one by one the many books of ancient wisdom she had sent. This extraordinary

8

woman expanded my cultural boundaries, and the new horizons exhilarated me. Rather than leaving me feeling utterly confused and fractured, these volumes became the welcome missing links in my education. Gobbling them up, I began to feel more whole, and I finished the lot by our departure.

On the porch of that log cabin in New Hampshire started a lifelong quest, a wondrous journey. Sitting there, alone, without a teacher or translator, I let this information wash over me. I absorbed it into my mind and heart as much as I could. In the thirty-plus years since that evening, I have continued to read Eastern philosophy, which has confirmed what I already suspected, that we will never know, understand or have a firm handle on truth. But we can make of this inner search a lifetime quest.

Over the years I've encountered many of you walking along this same path — this journey with no beginnings and no endings, during which we catch glimpses of wholeness, a wholeness that is really holiness.

What a great help these models have been to me! Several quotes, as well as some grace notes, are worth reading over and over. Like favorite hymns, they will become familiar and comfortable, useful, timely, and

♪·♪

uplifting. There are times when you feel a deep connection to something someone else says or expresses. Those thoughts seem more alive than reality. You say to yourself, "That's what I think." "That was written just for me." You suddenly feel an extraordinary surge of energy and experience increased capacity.

Dr. Johnson believes that we don't need to be informed, but reminded. Grace notes, like favorite quotations, will mean different things to you at different times in your life as your circumstances change. Some grace notes will be stimulating, some will be provocative, others will speak to you with a sense of urgency, while some may seem like a bland fortune in a Chinese cookie. Embrace them all as valid. Sometime, and perhaps now. When you read these messages, do so with the understanding that English forces us to choose a gender pronoun but that the underlying consciousness is of mankind, of humankind, all-embracing, and one.

Readers tell me that my grace notes give them energy, inspiration and ideas, often confirming and affirming their own values, tastes and style of living. Grace notes are a reminder that the way we are currently living could be improved by being totally present. Perhaps life isn't bad after all and can be made more satisfying and sacred by changing our attitudes, focusing our undivided attention even on the smallest tasks.

These simple random thoughts and uplifting quotations, insights, practical tips and suggestions may at best stir you into action but at the very least they may produce a sense of wonder. My hope is that they will inspire you to create your own grace notes and more grace in your daily rituals. Grace notes really are ours to share. Everything good and positive that broadens our appreciation and appetite for life is our lifetime goal.

Grace notes remind us that it is often the little things, the small revelations, that make a great deal of difference in handling disappointment, frustration and loss. They help us celebrate moments of joy by enabling us to unearth the underlying goodness of things.

As I sit by a warm fire in the living room of our dear Connecticut cottage preparing this little book I realize what immense joy I am experiencing in the company of souls from all over the world going back several thousand years. But I also find sweet, quiet enjoyment in my own thoughts about things that have touched my life with grace.

In a spirit of openness and grace, use this little

book in your own way. Open it up today and jump right in. Each day offers you a quotation to cherish and two of my grace notes. Now it's up to you: I've left space for your own grace notes. This is just the beginning. If you're in the mood, feel free to read a few weeks at a time, or stay in the day. Plan your grace ahead, if the spirit moves you, but above all be for yourself *now*.

It doesn't matter how you choose to use this book as long as you make it work uniquely for you. What's important is to feel that you're part of the flow of this universal energy. In the back is an index so you can refer back to specific topics and in looking over these pages, relive your past grace.

Whatever today brings, try to make the most of it, making it the best day you can. I hope you will fill the day with many magical moments and grace notes and remember that everywhere, all of us are struggling and striving to do the same. In Emerson's words we are seeking the divinities that are sitting disguised. Grace notes are multifaceted, rich. They are as scattered as shooting stars, as diverse as the sea and the sky. Some are wise and wonderful; some are intentionally vague and mysterious. Whether they are instructional, specific, questioning, inspiring or just plain fun, pay

12

attention to them and how you react to them each day. If we focus on these tiny drops, adding our own plink, plop, splash, here and there, together we can add a touch of joy, a little grace to a world that is, yes, filled with great joy but also with terrible sorrow. In the New Testament, Philippians 4:8 encourages us to think:

"Whatsoever things are true,
Whatsoever things are honest,
Whatsoever things are just,
Whatsoever things are pure,
Whatsoever things are lovely,
Whatsoever things are of good report:
If there be any virtue,
and if there be any praise,
Think on these things."

In the words and spirit of Mother Teresa, who once said she didn't do great things but little things with a great deal of love, I wish you grace-filled days and joy.

Alexandra Stoddard

Stonington Village

WINTER

❖

The life which is unexamined
is not worth living.

PLATO

Health enough to make work a pleasure,
Wealth enough to support your needs,
Strength enough to battle with difficulties and
   overcome them,
Grace enough to toil until good is accomplished,
Charity enough to see good in your neighbor,
Love enough to move you to be useful and
   helpful to others,
Faith enough to make real the things of God,
Hope enough to remove all anxious fears
   concerning the future.

— JOHANN WOLFGANG VON GOETHE

Every man must find his own philosophy....
his attitude toward life.

LIN YUTANG

◼ Resolve to live each day by the Golden Rule and
use this time of fresh beginnings for renewal and
enlightenment.

◼ Set aside some books you want to read. Make a
list in the order you feel they will be most useful to
you. Take notes on cards or in a notebook to keep
track of your journey.

YOUR GRACE NOTES:

◼ finish Buddha Bk: Crack, Quests, Cann
Visionary Eye, poetry- Passion
of W. Muriel

To be a philosopher is not merely to have subtle
thoughts....but so to love wisdom as to live according
to its dictates, a life of simplicity, independence,
magnanimity, and trust.

HENRY DAVID THOREAU

▨ Before the year's momentum builds, pause and
reflect: What do you need to do in order to make
the best and wisest use of your time, so that you
may live in harmony with your beliefs and ideals?

▨ Now is a good time to clean your home and
office of last year's clutter. Free yourself to be
independent.

YOUR GRACE NOTES:

▨ *Begin with Closets*
and attic

*H*ave patience with all things, but chiefly have
patience with yourself. Do not lose courage in
considering your own imperfections, but instantly
set about remedying them—every day begin
the task anew.

FRANCIS DE SALES

🔲 Make a pact with yourself, promising that you
will have realistic expectations. The art of living
takes time to develop and improvements will be
significant if you are kind to yourself.

🔲 Set aside time each day to be by yourself.
Let positive energy flow through you. Focus
on this message and really listen to it. Let it
become a part of you.

YOUR GRACE NOTES:

🔲 ....
....
....

I expect to pass through this world but once. Any good therefore that I can do, or any kindness that I can show to any fellow creature, let me do it now.

AUTHOR UNKNOWN

- We all give of ourselves uniquely. Do what is most natural, what you feel is most *you*.

- Call a friend today. Or write a postcard to someone you're thinking about. Do it now. Try to live each day doing for others something that also enriches you.

YOUR GRACE NOTES:

- Make one call a day
  or a note
  I need to work our a
  deepened generosity
  to everyone

*H*ow often things occur by mere chance
which we dare not even hope for.

TERENCE

■ When Peter married me he told me there
would be many surprises. Be receptive and
open to recognize these blessings.

■ Consider jotting down these serendipitous
occurrences. Let them be the beginning of a
long gratitude list.

YOUR GRACE NOTES:

■ *Fr. Bill - the integrity he brought*
to his work - his love of history
Fr. Marshall - travel - Music
of Mozart - Gilbert - Sullivan -
Church calendar hymns

*I*n order to carry out great enterprises,
one must live as if one will never have to die.

MARQUIS DE VAUVENARGUES

🔳 The people who inspire us the most are those who
plant trees they will never see mature, and who
live at full tilt every day, even on the day they die.

🔳 Dream big dreams. If you are considering writing
an article, develop it into a book. If you are writing
a book, think ahead to your next project. Fill your
days with ambitious goals.

YOUR GRACE NOTES:

🔳 *Today Asst. Dir –*
Tomorrow Dir

*T*he one fact that I would cry from every housetop is
this: the Good Life is waiting for us — here and now!
.... At this very moment we have the necessary
techniques, both material and psychological, to
create a full and satisfying life for everyone.

B. F. SKINNER

■ All we will ever experience is the present moment
as we live it. Each moment is a microcosm of our
whole life, who we are.

■ Take two minutes to breathe deeply and realize
that tomorrow will not be better than today as if
by magic. Where we are now is what we have to
work with and *is* "the Good Life."

YOUR GRACE NOTES:

■ This certainly fits in w.
Sarah's visit & the
she gave me to read
Chumpra

23

The warm familiar sense of my own existence,
with all its exasperation, all its charm.

LOGAN PEARSALL SMITH

▦ Embrace every minute because they are all
interconnected, one with the other. They're yours.
This is your autobiography.

▦ Use your energy positively. While you're going
through a frustrating time, isolate each problem so
you may get back on track.

YOUR GRACE NOTES:

▦ ....
....
....
....
....

*T*he most certain sign of wisdom
is a continual cheerfulness…
MICHEL DE MONTAIGNE

- When you're centered in the flow of your life you will experience contentment. You don't have power over what happens but you can control ✓ your attitude.

- Whenever you feel really upset, analyze why and don't blame yourself. You can live with yourself a great deal better when you have a good disposition. Have a cookie and a cup of tea and spend a few minutes nurturing yourself. ✓

YOUR GRACE NOTES:

- *Buddha wd. agree w. MonTaigne*

....

....

*T*he most beautiful thing we can experience
is the mysterious.

ALBERT EINSTEIN

※ Even a genius doesn't have all the answers. No one ever does. Keep moving in the direction of your goals. Some minor mysteries do get resolved.

※ Listen to the stirrings of your heart. Pay attention to your intuitions. Carry on a silent conversation with yourself. Don't question everything but accept the good and run with it.

YOUR GRACE NOTES:

※ *Appropo for ME right now. I feel as though I were flying by my intuitions*

26

*M*an's happiness in life is the result
of man's own effort....

CH'EN TU-HSIU

■ Happiness is a by-product of a thoughtful,
disciplined life. Aim at fulfilling whatever talents
you have inherited and develop yourself to your
fullest potential.

■ Take some psychological
tests to determine your
skills and put the pieces
of the puzzle together to
build on your strengths.

YOUR GRACE NOTES:

■ *This fits in with my*
Wondteep to stretch
Repair now —
develop new parts
of me — I think I
Can — I think I Can

*C*uriosity is one of the permanent and certain
characteristics of a vigorous intellect.

SAMUEL JOHNSON

▦ The best way to enrich your knowledge and
understanding of the mysteries of life is to be
inquisitive. Ask many questions. Do not assume
you know the answers.

▦ Once you find you are interested in a subject,
attack it. Go to the library and become a student.
Knowledge is accumulated incrementally,
each day.

YOUR GRACE NOTES:

▦ ....
....
....

*L*ife is a pure flame, and we live by
an invisible sun within us.

SIR THOMAS BROWNE

- The storms of life don't have to get inside us. A professor from Yale, William Lyon Phelps, advised his students to paint the walls of their minds with many beautiful pictures.

- Carry your light with you wherever you are. In difficult moments, visualize a favorite place — a beach or a mountaintop. Keep this image until you are one with nature. Let yourself be transported to that beautiful spot.

YOUR GRACE NOTES:

....
....
....

29

*L*ost time is never found again.
BENJAMIN FRANKLIN

▧   Learn to live by the motto "Do it now." Never say
to yourself or anyone else, "I've had a bad day."
You'll never be able to go back and fix it. Make the
best of all times.

▧   Stargazing, doing nothing, is not "lost time."
"Lost time" is time you waste in negative thoughts.
When you feel stuck, change your mood with some
physical exercise. Don't brood and let time drift
by unproductively.

YOUR GRACE NOTES:

▧   ....
....
....
....
....

Tomorrow's life is too late. Live today.

MARTIAL

☒ Future plans shouldn't preclude you from living fully now. If today is all you'll ever have, live it in a way that best expresses your love of life.

☒ Each day concentrate on every single thing you do. This way, if there is a tomorrow, you can do the same. Each day you wake up, pretend that your lifetime has to be lived in this day. It works!

YOUR GRACE NOTES:

☒ ....
....
....
....

*A*ction! Action! Action!

DEMOSTHENES

⊠ Aristotle teaches us about active virtue. Once you have a clear vision of the right thing to do, move your feet.

⊠ Each day, jot down the little things you want to accomplish as well as your long-range goals. In this way, all your efforts will be focused in the right direction.

YOUR GRACE NOTES:

⊠ ....
....
....
....
....
....

*A*ny disaster you can survive is an improvement
in your character, your stature, and your life.
What a privilege!

JOSEPH CAMPBELL

People who survive horrible events are best
able to help others to cope until they too
become survivors.

When your inner resources are
challenged, remember those you
admire whose courage and strength
are an inspiration to you. Be brave
and you will find strength.

YOUR GRACE NOTES:

....
....
....
....
....
....
....
....
....
....

*N*o man is happy who does not think himself so.

PUBLILIUS SYRUS

■ By appreciating all the good times, all the fun moments, you live in the consciousness of a pleasant life. Be determined to live a happy life and no one will take it away from you.

■ To a greater degree than you might be aware, each of us has to determine just how happy we choose to be.

YOUR GRACE NOTES:

■ ....
....
....
....
....
....

*C*ulture is to know the best that has been said
and thought in the world.

MATTHEW ARNOLD

🔲 Life is far too short to ever know enough. The
only way to gain knowledge is to have a steady
diet of good (not escapist) literature.

🔲 Anytime a writer "speaks to you," read anything
by that author you can. If necessary, ask someone
to do a search for you in a used bookstore. You'll
discover a reason for the connection — in time.

YOUR GRACE NOTES:

🔲 ....
....
....
....
....

35

To be what we are, and to become what we are
capable of becoming, is the only end of life.

ROBERT LOUIS STEVENSON

◼ All that is expected is for us to be ourselves.
Whenever we are true to our selves and live by
our intuitive nature, we rely on our strengths, not
our shortcomings.

◼ Without telling anyone, write a personal statement
about your life and what your goals are for the
months ahead. Tuck it in your wallet.

YOUR GRACE NOTES:

◼ ....
   ....
   ....

To know what we do not know
is the beginning of wisdom.

MAHA STHAVIRA SANGHARAKSHITA

■ Wise men and women have an insatiable thirst for knowledge. It is this energy for life that ultimately makes someone wise.

■ Play a game with yourself. The rule is: Don't assume anything. See everything as though for the first time. As you eliminate prejudices and labels, new insights will begin to emerge.

YOUR GRACE NOTES:

■ ....
....
....
....
....
....
....

*K*nowledge is the antidote to fear.
RALPH WALDO EMERSON

- When we know, we have more courage.

- In his Inaugural Address, Franklin Delano Roosevelt said, "The only thing we have to fear is fear itself." Once we know the facts, no matter how brutally painful they often are, we can make intelligent decisions.

- Self-knowledge is the key. If you don't deceive yourself you are more likely to get to the truth. At the end of this day, rate yourself from one to ten on how truthful you've been. Fear increases with deceit.

YOUR GRACE NOTES:

- ....
....
....

A single conversation across the table with a wise
man is better than ten years' study of books.

HENRY WADSWORTH LONGFELLOW

■ Whenever you are in the company of a superior
communicator, feel that energy flow through
you. Participate and interact at a high level of
concentration as well as enjoyment.

■ Most everyone has a really interesting story to
tell and it's there for the asking. Ask questions
that will encourage another person to open up
and let you in on their excitement about life.
Think: "Enough about me. I want to learn
about you."

YOUR GRACE NOTES:

■ ....
....
....

A good character carries with it the highest power
of causing a thing to be believed.

ARISTOTLE

■ No one ever said life wouldn't be complicated.
Associate yourself only with trustworthy people,
even if this requires some tough choices involving
family and friends.

■ Write down all the people in your life who have
let you down or cheated you in any way. Now take
this piece of paper and burn it. Let go.

YOUR GRACE NOTES:

■ ....
....
....
....
....

*Z*en teaches nothing; it merely enables us to wake up
and become aware. It does not teach, it points.

D. T. SUZUKI

※ Running around stressed-out and aggravated
indicates that you are out of control. Zen will
bring perspective to life and death by illuminating
your ability to pay attention to everything with
equal force.

※ Take a yoga class or begin daily meditation.
Read a few books on Zen and Tao so you can
be pointed in the direction of enlightenment.
Consider going to a retreat. Ask a spiritual adviser
for information.

YOUR GRACE NOTES:

※ ....
....
....

41

..... *A* heart that lives in grace....

DANTE

🔲 Living well is a courageous act and is our greatest
achievement. Grace can enter our souls only when
we stop trying to control the uncontrollable —
nature and others!

🔲 Think of your friends and acquaintances as "grace
bearers" the way my friend and spiritual mentor
John Bowen Coburn does.

🔲 Think about these people as you go about your
day and concentrate on why you think they have
hearts full of grace.

YOUR GRACE NOTES:

🔲 ....
....
....

*S*orrow shared is halved and joy shared is doubled.
NATIVE AMERICAN SAYING

▣ Love always eases pain. The mere presence of
family and friends at sad times will help you
begin to heal. Sharing happiness can become a
way of life.

▣ There are times and places when solitude is timely.
Remember, however, that sad times, when you
are tempted to isolate yourself, can be alleviated
when shared. Celebrations should be an exchange
of positive energy between you and others. The
right chemistry can create joy: mysterious grace
that just happens.

YOUR GRACE NOTES:

▣ ....
....
....

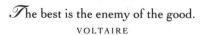

The best is the enemy of the good.
VOLTAIRE

- ❊ Once you know the difference between all right and exceptional, all right no longer seems good enough.

- ❊ When you do your best, you know it. Strive to do your best every time and then let go. Sometimes you will be only good, "all right," and that's okay. Trying is the point.

YOUR GRACE NOTES:

❊ ....
....
....
....

*O*ut of your vulnerabilities will come your strength.

SIGMUND FREUD

🔲 We will become strong only after we have
acknowledged our weaknesses.

🔲 Aim at becoming more sensitive to your
vulnerabilities and you will find the necessary
strength to accept them.

YOUR GRACE NOTES:

🔲 ....
....
....
....
....
....
....
....

*Y*our closest relationships seem to matter
most for your health.

DR. JANICE KIECOLT-GLASER

- The people nearest you have the greatest hold
  over your well-being. Select them with great care
  because they make a great deal of difference —
  even to your immune system.

- Don't fight back. It's better to go for a long walk
  than raise your blood pressure. You are in control
  of how you respond to the behavior of others, not
  how well or badly others behave.

YOUR GRACE NOTES:

....
....
....

I am still learning.

MICHELANGELO

▨ Peter wants his tombstone to read "Still learning."
The more deeply we delve into the history of
civilization, the less bothered we ought to be about
the little stuff. Be a student of life.

 ▨ What do you want to learn today? What's stopping
you? Begin. By tomorrow when you're beginning
a new month, you'll be in the flow.

YOUR GRACE NOTES:

▨ ....
....
....
....
....
....
....

In comparing various authors with one another,
I have discovered that some of the greatest and latest
writers have transcribed, word for word, from former
works, without making acknowledgment.

PLINY THE ELDER

⊠ Whenever we read something that touches us,
we tend to remember it unconsciously or
subconsciously. We are not always aware how
these words came to us.

⊠ Always credit someone when you're aware
of your source of inspiration. It never hurts you
and it flatters others.

YOUR GRACE NOTES:

⊠ ....
....
....
....

I searched through rebellion, drugs, diets, mysticism, religions, intellectualisms, and much more, only to begin to find....that truth is basically simple — and feels good, clear and right.

CHICK COREA

▣ Truth is always available to the seeker. You know when something is true because you feel it viscerally.

▣ Be a truth seeker. It saves you from life-threatening detours and is a worthy companion in good and bad times.

YOUR GRACE NOTES:

▣ ....
....
....
....

... *It* is pointless to praise the light and preach it if nobody can see it. It is much more needful to teach people the art of seeing.... In order to facilitate this inner vision we must first clear the way for the faculty of seeing. How this is to be done without psychology....is, frankly, beyond my comprehension.

CARL JUNG

▣ By concentrating on even the smallest elements of our lives we see that we are part of a greater wholeness. When we try to take care of the smallest things, the deepening process begins.

▣ Keep a daily log of all the wonders you experience in nature as well as the beautiful encounters you have with those around you.

YOUR GRACE NOTES:

▣ ....
....
....
....
....

...*A*ll noble things are as difficult as they are rare.

SPINOZA

- Everyone expects life to be easy. Scott Peck opened his best-selling book *The Road Less Traveled* with "Life is difficult."

- Ease and depth don't usually go together. Accept that everything worthwhile is challenging. Then you will have greater moments of grace because you will be prepared.

YOUR GRACE NOTES:

- ....
....
....
....
....

*C*onscience is an instinct to judge ourselves in
the light of moral laws. It is not a mere faculty; it
is an instinct.

IMMANUEL KANT

■ We always know. Trust your ability to recognize
your instinct as truth.

 ■ We can all be wise when we live our lives
backward. When you are uncomfortable about
a situation, pay attention. Your instincts are telling
you to listen *before* you act.

YOUR GRACE NOTES:

■ ....
....
....
....
....

*T*ruths kindle light for truths.

JULIUS CAESAR

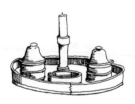

- ▧ Think of the times when you have been totally honest with yourself and remember how calm you felt.

- ▧ There is no such thing as a partial truth. Catch yourself and correct your fabrications. When you're with a friend and something sounds odd, inquire, "Is that what you really think?"

YOUR GRACE NOTES:

▧ ....
....
....
....
....

*L*earning is a name superior to beauty; learning
is better than hidden treasure....learning is
strength inexhaustible.

THE HITOPADESA

🔲 Imagine all the useful information we could
accumulate over a lifetime if we kept an open
mind to all different points of view. Do!

🔲 We learn by doing. No matter how much we learn
from others, the best way to know is to experience
everything firsthand, so long as the experience is
life-enhancing, not dangerous or illegal.

YOUR GRACE NOTES:

🔲 ....
....
....

*L*ife is half spent before we know what it is.
GEORGE HERBERT

▣ Remember the writing on the Chinese wall: "It's later than you think." For each of us, today is the beginning of the rest of our lives; it is and always has been.

▣ To avoid "what might have been," the saddest words in any language, start now to determine what's most important to *you.* Live it now.

YOUR GRACE NOTES:

▣ ....
....
....
....
....
....
....

*I*n truth, prosperity tries the souls even of the wise.

SALLUST

- Don't abuse money. Don't overestimate what it can do for you. It can buy you time, and for that alone be grateful.

- No one has ever been wise who used money as power. Have you ever considered giving anonymously?

YOUR GRACE NOTES:

- ....
  ....
  ....
  ....
  ....
  ....
  ....

To rejoice in life, to find the world beautiful and
delightful to live in, was a mark of the Greek spirit
which distinguished it from all that had gone before.
It is a vital distinction.

EDITH HAMILTON

■ The ancient Greeks illuminated the way. They
strove for beauty and grace in all aspects of life.
Beauty is a better ideal to focus on than the dark
side of human nature.

■ Read *The Greek Way* by Edith
Hamilton and you too will feel
like rejoicing.

YOUR GRACE NOTES:

■ *It is a powerful boat*

....
....
....
....
....
....
....

57

It is only by risking from one hour to another
that we live at all.

WILLIAM JAMES

🖼 We should always try to enlarge our envelope —
stretching beyond what is comfortable. Soon we
will have manicured the wilderness.

🖼 Try something new. If you've always roasted lamb
a certain way, experiment with a new recipe. Try
studding a leg of lamb with garlic and marinating
it with honey, teriyaki sauce and rosemary. Every
new opportunity is a chance to experiment.

YOUR GRACE NOTES:

🖼 ....
....
....

*O*ne thing leads to another.

JUDGE J. EDWARD LUMBARD

■ Nothing exists in isolation. Go and keep on going. Everything will come together in accomplishment, pleasure and satisfaction when you stick with something.

■ Go the extra mile!

YOUR GRACE NOTES:

■ ....
....
....
....
....
....

*O*ne word frees us of all the weight and pain of life:
That word is love.

SOPHOCLES

■ To receive love, be loving.

■ What a world we could celebrate if we could
learn to love one another. Try, and the world will
go around!

YOUR GRACE NOTES:

■ ....
....
....
....
....
....
....
....

Love conquers all things;
let us too surrender to Love.

VIRGIL

▓ Love is expressed in our tone of voice, in a smile,
in our ability to look and listen to another and in
our desire for romance.

▓ When we surrender to love, we lose our
self-centeredness and surge toward those we love.

YOUR GRACE NOTES:

▓ ....
....
....
....
....
....
....
....

Joy is an achievement; it presupposes an inner effort, that of productive activity.

ERICH FROMM

■ Joy is a result, not a goal. Work hard. Live life to the fullest and there is a possibility that you will have many joy-filled moments of indescribable beauty. The harder you work, the more there is a chance for joy.

■ When joy enters your life, celebrate it and live it as fully as you can. When sorrow comes, remember that you have experienced joy and will again.

YOUR GRACE NOTES:

■ ....
....
....
....
....

True words always seem paradoxical but no other
form of teaching can take its place.

LAO-TZU

- Life is constant flux. There is good news and bad
  news. By understanding what to focus on you can
  learn the subtle art of living.

- Read *Tao-te Ching*. Lao-tzu teaches us about our
  nature through nature, with its storms and its
  balmy, sunny days. There is no perfection, but we
  can learn to appreciate the beauty of what we are
  capable of comprehending.

YOUR GRACE NOTES:

- ....
  ....
  ....

*R*ule your mind or it will rule you.

HORACE

◾ Control the menu of thoughts and images that flash through your mind. Dwell on all the positive, affirmative things in your life, and they will become your inspiration.

◾ Whenever your mind tries to dwell on negative information, take time to sit quietly and silently clear your head. Think of a clear, flowing brook with fresh water gently cleansing and refreshing you until you feel calm and renewed.

YOUR GRACE NOTES:

◾
....
....
....
....
....
....

*A*ll thoughts, all passions, all delights,
Whatever stirs this mortal frame,
All are but ministers of Love,
And feed his sacred flame.

SAMUEL TAYLOR COLERIDGE

■ Everything you think affects your spirit, your
mood and your ability to contribute to others.

■ It is hard to feel love and hate at the same time
even though both exist. Concentrate on loving
thoughts; they will lift you up. Whatever your
immediate circumstances — there are always
plenty of things and people to love.

YOUR GRACE NOTES:

■ ....
....
....

*O*ne of the best things about love is just recognizing a man's step when he climbs the stairs.

COLETTE

■ One of the joys of finally living in a house is to have stairs. When Peter comes up the stairs, I look up with pleasure. Love's music plays many varied tunes.

■ When someone you love comes up the stairs, isn't that cause for celebration? "Hey hey, ho ho." It's these little rituals that reinforce the fact that we are loved.

YOUR GRACE NOTES:

■ ....
....
....
....

The time which we have at our disposal every day is
elastic; the passions that we feel expand it, those that
we inspire contract it; and habit fills up what remains.

MARCEL PROUST

▨ Time is a resource to be used creatively,
inventively and imaginatively. Be sure you have
more and more passions to expand it. What
inspires you will take up most of your time and
will leave little for routine habits which aren't that
important.

▨ Divide each day into sections. Do creative work
before your habitual chores. While you do your
necessary work you will enjoy it because you
will have first satisfied yourself. Create first, then
clean up.

YOUR GRACE NOTES:

▨ ....
   ....
   ....

God helps them that help themselves.

BENJAMIN FRANKLIN

- Ultimately, no one else has the answers to your unique set of circumstances. You know best and are the one who must take the necessary steps toward self-improvement.

- Take responsibility for your life. Whatever happened in the past is dead. No one else can be another person's savior. To save one life is a victory; we must begin with our own.

YOUR GRACE NOTES:

....
....
....
....
....

*N*ever give way to melancholy; resist it steadily,
for the habit will encroach.

SYDNEY SMITH

▦ Mood patterns become habitually good or bad.
Choose to look at the bright side of life while
you're alive because the darkness is nearer than
any one of us has the capacity of knowing.

▦ Whenever we turn inward and feel sorry for
ourselves, we find it hard to get out of our own
way. Go volunteer at a soup kitchen or work in a
hospital. Change bedpans for AIDS victims and
you'll be cured quickly. You don't have to travel
far to help someone who is *really* desperate.

YOUR GRACE NOTES:

▦ ....
....
....

A light broke in upon my brain —....
The sweetest song ear ever heard.
LORD BYRON

- Suddenly, as if out of the sky, you understand and everything seems to lighten up and make sense. In these moments you realize all your thoughtfulness was not lost, but was the seed for harmony.

- Get ready; a light is about to go off. See and experience all its luminosity.

YOUR GRACE NOTES:

....
....
....
....

To know when one's self is interested,
is the first condition of interesting other people.

WALTER PATER

- Enthusiasm is never an orphan; it multiplies.
- What are you the most excited about right now? Your recommendation has weight when you care to spread the word.

YOUR GRACE NOTES:

- ....
....
....
....
....
....
....

*O*ur concern be peace of mind....
keep unlovely things afar.

THEOCRITUS

- I'm never receptive to inspiration
  and creative thoughts until I've
  cleansed my mind of all the
  clutter, the stuff that does no one
  any good.

- If you can't think of someone
  lovingly, far better to blank that
  person out of your mind. You may never be able to
  be at peace with that person but you are always in
  control of maintaining a peaceful spirit.

YOUR GRACE NOTES:

- ....
  ....
  ....
  ....
  ....
  ....
  ....
  ....

The least initial deviation from the truth
is multiplied later a thousandfold.

ARISTOTLE

■ The definition of sin is to go off the path. Truth is
experienced in everything we do as we go through
the day. If we ever shade the truth partially, it is a
bad signal. Truth rings true.

■ If you've ever told a lie, you suffer far more than
the person to whom you told it. Why suffer?
Let's analyze what possible reasons could cause
us to dissemble, then move back to our center.
What is, is.

YOUR GRACE NOTES:

■ ....
....
....

The stream of time is carrying us forward;
we live between yesterday and tomorrow.

LIN YUTANG

🔲 Nature teaches us about change and that we must
be flexible in order to survive. Nothing stays the
same, which reminds us of the limits of time.

🔲 Think about what you want to be doing in five
years. How old will you be? What would you like
to be doing in ten years? Where do you want to
live? Hurry!

YOUR GRACE NOTES:

🔲 ....
....
....
....
....
....

That is the happiest conversation where there is no competition, no vanity, but a calm, quiet interchange of sentiments.

SAMUEL JOHNSON

- When you have nothing to prove, you can enrich the time shared with your friends by being attentive, open, sympathetic and loving.

- The greatest honor friends can pay you is to tell you about something good that happened to them. If you're not envious or jealous, you will be deeply touched.

YOUR GRACE NOTES:

- ....
....
....

*T*hat life is worth living
is the most necessary of assumptions....

GEORGE SANTAYANA

- This is it. There is no other possible life. We have to work with what we have and make our efforts worthy, and if we're fortunate, they'll have lasting power.

- The best way to confirm your belief in the value of life is to experience the bravery of people who struggle for mere survival.

YOUR GRACE NOTES:

- ....
....
....

A good listener is not only popular everywhere,
but after a while he knows something.

WILSON MIZNER

■ It's true. We don't learn *anything* new when we're
speaking. Unless you have something you want to
communicate, listening will enrich you much more
than trying to entertain others.

■ Practice listening.

YOUR GRACE NOTES:

■ ....
....
....
....
....
....
....

*D*raw from others the lesson
that may profit yourself.

TERENCE

- Anyone who brings something constructive to
  your life is a role model. Look for the lessons
  others have to teach you.

- If you have learned something of significance
  from someone, reach out to that person and say
  thank you.

YOUR GRACE NOTES:

- ....
  ....
  ....
  ....
  ....

....*To* be alive means to be productive, to use one's powers not for any purpose transcending man, but for oneself, to make sense of one's existence, to be human. As long as anyone believes that his ideal and purpose is outside himself, that it is above the clouds, in the past or in the future, he will go outside himself and seek fulfillment where it can not be found. He will look for solutions and answers at every point except the one where they can be found — in himself.

ERICH FROMM

◼ We have to live our lives now, not save ourselves for a future journey. Look for clues from within; you need to cope with one world: yours.

◼ Live *your* life. No one else can do it but you. There is no one like you — never has been. Write a poem, for you. Sing a song, for you. Climb a mountain, for you. Cook a stew, for you....

YOUR GRACE NOTES:

◼ ....
....

*L*ife in March weather, savage
and serene in one hour.
RALPH WALDO EMERSON

⊠ This morning we had a severe storm and by
afternoon a most elegant sunset over calm water.
We're all like the weather — we change. But we
have control over our emotions no matter what is
going on inside us.

⊠ Hug it all — if the weather is *really* awful, sit by a
warm fire and sip hot cinnamon tea as you listen to
Danny Wright at the piano, on tape.

YOUR GRACE NOTES:

⊠ ....
....
....

*Give us grace and strength to forbear
and to persevere....give us courage....
and the quiet mind....*

ROBERT LOUIS STEVENSON

- A walk in the woods, or experiencing nature in all her majesty, often invigorates us when we are afraid.

- Once we accept that the worst thing that can happen to us is death, then we can be calm and go about the business of life. Live with the idea that you must continuously work on your unfinished business. What is yours today?

YOUR GRACE NOTES:

- ....
....

Taste is nothing but a delicate good sense.

M. J. DE CHÉNIER

◪ Remember the triangle of simplicity, appropriateness and beauty — it will never fail you.

◪ What have you recently discovered about your likes and preferences that brings greater pleasure to your life? Photography?

YOUR GRACE NOTES:

◪

....
....
....
....
....
....
....

It takes a long time to bring
excellence to maturity.
PUBLILIUS SYRUS

■ We should be patient in steadily working toward
our goals. Perhaps what we want to express will
require a lifetime of work to make it good enough
and worthy of recognition.

■ Go for it. Believe in yourself with all your
tenacity. Do it for yourself because this is the
only way to light a dark corner.

YOUR GRACE NOTES:

■ ....
....
....
....

83

I try to catch every sentence,
every word you and I say....
ANTON CHEKHOV

■ Treasure magical moments. You can carry them
with you wherever you are, forever.

■ Write in a journal the essence of special
conversations in order to treasure them for all
time. You live twice as deeply when you record
your affirmations.

YOUR GRACE NOTES:

■
....
....
....
....
....

*O*mit needless words.
WILLIAM STRUNK, JR.

- We don't have to be wordy in order to make a point. In life, everything is strengthened when we are direct. Speak your heart plainly.

- Everyone is in a hurry. A few quick words will always be appreciated. The sooner, the shorter.

YOUR GRACE NOTES:

....
....
....
....
....
....
....
....
....
....
....

*K*eep the faculty of effort alive in you
by a little gratuitous exercise every day.

WILLIAM JAMES

▩   A few tummy tucks a day, while meditating, a few
stretches, while listening to music, will give you a
sense of control as you face the challenges of the
unknown.

▩   Swim for exercise, dance for romance. Movement
is key. Have fun!

YOUR GRACE NOTES:

▩   ....
....
....
....
....
....
....

We never know how high we are
Till we are called to rise.

EMILY DICKINSON

- Never say you can't do something. It is a lie.

- What is the biggest challenge facing you now?
  Hold on. You can be brave.
  You're almost there.
  Never give up.

YOUR GRACE NOTES:

....
....
....
....
....
....
....
....
....

*H*old faithfulness and sincerity
as first principles.

CONFUCIUS

⊠ Whenever you are true to yourself, you will also
be true to others.

⊠ Think about faithfulness and sincerity and how
they affect your life. If someone were unfaithful
and insincere with you, what would your reaction
be? Go for a walk and think about it.

YOUR GRACE NOTES:

⊠ ....
....
....
....
....

Learning to live is learning to let go.

SOGYAL RINPOCHE

■ Whenever we cling too tightly to anything, we become uptight and so do the people around us. Change is the only promise life holds. Flow with life.

■ What are you anxious about that is causing you stress? Nothing lasts forever. Whenever you let go you become open and free to receive something new, something unknown to you now. When you let go, you lose pain and gain insight.

YOUR GRACE NOTES:

■ ....
....

*T*ruth is on the march and nothing can stop it.
ÉMILE ZOLA

🔲 March along with truth and you'll be the hit of
the parade.

🔲 Truth is liberating. If you have something
serious on your mind, tell someone who can keep
a confidence or write it in your journal. The next
step is to live this truth, starting now.

YOUR GRACE NOTES:

🔲 ....
....
....
....
....
....
....
....

*A*ll intellectual improvement arises from leisure.

SAMUEL JOHNSON

🔲 Your free time should be divided between mental and physical disciplines. By sheer determination, you can improve your mind. Some of your leisure time should be spent educating yourself.

🔲 If you can't find one hour a day to read, reflect, create and leisurely putter, you should make some changes in your life. No thinking person can live well without reading and time for reflection. Write down how much television you watched this past week. There you go!

YOUR GRACE NOTES:

🔲 ....
....
....
....

91

There is no substitute for hard work.

THOMAS ALVA EDISON

I love to work. I enjoy the physicalness of everything I do. Simply pressing buttons makes me crazy. Whenever I do something that requires mental or physical effort, I feel exhilarated.

What is your private work, the project you're doing for you and no one else? How long have you been at it? I realized I was a writer when I finished my first book. After I turned it in to the publisher I sat at my desk and took notes and began to write my next book. What do you do for yourself? What are *you* passionate about?

YOUR GRACE NOTES:

....
....
....

*N*ever despair.
HORACE

*N*ever, never.
WINSTON CHURCHILL

🔳 First, be kind to yourself. Then, be tough. Be a fighter. Be a survivor. Always get back up on the horse.

🔳 Don't quit before the finish line. Walking away from something that is bad for you is not quitting.

YOUR GRACE NOTES:

🔳 ....
....
....
....
....
....

The first and the simplest emotion
which we discover in the human mind is curiosity.

EDMUND BURKE

◻ Wouldn't it be wonderful if you could remain as
curious as a three-year-old child?

◻ If you are a member of a religious organization
and have firm beliefs, spend a month visiting and
participating in other worship services. You can
increase your inspiration for life a thousandfold by
being curious and embracing it all.

YOUR GRACE NOTES:

◻ ....
....
....
....
....
....
....

*T*here are occasions when it is undoubtedly
better to incur loss than to make gain.

TITUS MACCIUS PLAUTUS

■ Only you know all the circumstances surrounding
your decisions. You're allowed to make mistakes.
We all do. Move forward in the direction of
your convictions. You can't always see how far
you've come.

■ Winning is the result of a process. It's how
you play the game that matters. Far better to be
honest, fair and kind as you move along than to
make big gains at the expense of other people's
dignity or security.

YOUR GRACE NOTES:

■   ....
    ....

>...*L*et him cry whoever feels like crying....
>the shedding of a tear, whether of forgiveness or
>of pity or of sheer delight at beauty,
>will do him a lot of good.

LIN YUTANG

When Mrs. Brown finally died just before her
101st birthday, I called a close friend. Once I
heard his voice I began to cry and was too choked
up to talk. I loved Mrs. Brown. Crying helped. So
did my friend John, who listened as I cried. I cry
often. It's okay to cry.

Think of crying as singing. You
wouldn't want to keep a song inside
when you had an urge to sing.
Crying reminds us that we're moved
by life's sorrows and beauties and
we're participating in them all fully.

YOUR GRACE NOTES:

....
....
....

*Y*ou have to take time to live.
Living takes time.

ELEANOR MCMILLEN BROWN

▣ Mrs. Brown lived an elegant, disciplined,
determined life as the doyenne of interior design.
She never overdid; she never had to. She took her
time and God gave her plenty of time to do what
was useful.

▣ Unless you enjoy your work and do it with
pleasure, you will feel frustration and a sense
of hopelessness. Who is it who puts too much
pressure on you? Why are you allowing someone
to demand more of you than your best? Why?
"Living takes time."

YOUR GRACE NOTES:

▣ ....
....

*T*here is no excellent beauty that hath not some
strangeness in the proportion.

FRANCIS BACON

◪ Look for the character and authenticity of beauty.
The Japanese believe beauty should have a flaw to
be alive. Excellence is never perfect; it is merely
excellent.

◪ Try seeing your everyday surroundings
differently. Perfect symmetry can be frightfully
dull. Loosen things up and create a bit of
strangeness that will add interest.

YOUR GRACE NOTES:

◪ ....
....
....
....
....
....

To see a World in a Grain of Sand,
And a Heaven in a Wild Flower,
Hold Infinity in the palm of your hand,
And Eternity in an hour.

WILLIAM BLAKE

When we can take a close look at the wonders in our midst right now, today, here, we begin to feel the muse that inspires poets. It's all here; it's up to us to become more keenly aware.

Examine everything as if you have just taken off blinders. Really look at the tomato you are slicing and the soap bubbles in the kitchen sink. By magnifying the details, we gain perspective.

YOUR GRACE NOTES:

....
....
....
....
....

There are three marks of a superior man:
being virtuous, he is free from anxiety;
being wise, he is free from perplexity;
being brave, he is free from fear.

CONFUCIUS

🔳 The wise guide and teach us. When we do the
right thing, are discerning and tough, we are free
to live fully and well.

🔳 What are some steps you're taking to free yourself
from anxiety, perplexity and fear? Examine the
quality of the books you have on your bedside
table. By changing the thrust of your reading,
you can change your awareness.

YOUR GRACE NOTES:

🔳 ....
....
....

*D*o you know what those people are doing, boys?
Fertilizing daffodils!

ROBIN WILLIAMS as
Mr. Keating in *Dead Poets Society*

⊠ Vincent van Gogh wrote his brother Theo that
the time for work is short. So true. Everyone has
to find out what's really important and then get
down to it.

⊠ Rent the movie *Dead Poets Society* and have a
couple over for pea soup and salad and watch the
movie together.

YOUR GRACE NOTES:

⊠ ....
....
....
....
....

*T*ime cools, time clarifies; no mood can
be maintained quite unaltered through
the course of hours.

CARL JUNG

◼ Moods swing like a seesaw throughout the day.
Focus on the big picture; it will hold up well
against the test of time.

◼ If you are upset and feel like venting your
frustration, let it pour out on paper; don't get
on the telephone.

YOUR GRACE NOTES:

◼ ....
....
....
....
....
....

Just remain in the center, watching.
And then forget that you are there.

LAO-TZU

🔲 Practice losing your self-consciousness so that you
may be open to unencumbered awareness.

🔲 Whenever we forget about ourselves and go about
our work we are living beautifully. Get out of your
own way!

YOUR GRACE NOTES:

🔲 ....
....
....
....
....
....

*A*ll aglow in the work.

VIRGIL

- Self-expression, doing something of significance, is a powerful human urge. What makes you all aglow?

- What projects are you thinking of starting this Spring? What seeds have you planted that will bear fruit? Are you the lucky one who would be doing the same work even without pay?

YOUR GRACE NOTES:

- ....
....
....
....
....

MARCH 30

*W*here is human nature so weak
as in the bookstore!

HENRY WARD BEECHER

▨ Books are spiritual food and are as important to
our well-ness as food and shelter. The books in
your library are friends who will always be there
in times of need.

▨ Make a list of the books you intend to read this
Spring. If you have a friend who enjoys the same
kinds of books you do, you can meet once a month
to discuss them — a bookclub of two!

YOUR GRACE NOTE*S*:

▨ ....
....

The world, — this shadow of the soul,
or *other me*, — lies wide around. Its attractions
are the keys which unlock my thoughts
and make me acquainted with myself.

RALPH WALDO EMERSON

We are an intricate, vital part of a larger harmony.
The world teaches us that our life matters.

When do you feel you are most in touch with your
spirit, the core of your being? Where are you?
What are you doing? Who are you with? Who
would you want to be with? How does this make
you feel?

YOUR GRACE NOTES:

....
....
....

Life is an opportunity, benefit from it.
Life is a beauty, admire it.
Life is bliss, taste it.
Life is a dream, realize it.
Life is a challenge, meet it.
Life is a duty, complete it.
Life is a game, play it.
Life is costly, care for it.
Life is wealth, keep it.
Life is love, enjoy it.
Life is mystery, know it.
Life is a promise, fulfill it.
Life is sorrow, overcome it.
Life is a song, sing it.
Life is a struggle, accept it.
Life is a tragedy, confront it.
Life is an adventure, dare it.
Life is luck, make it.
Life is too precious, do not destroy it.
Life is life, fight for it!

— MOTHER TERESA

$\mathscr{S}$PRING

❖

It is better to ask some questions
than to know all the answers.

JAMES THURBER

My Symphony of Life

To live content with small means;
to seek elegance rather than luxury, and
refinement rather than fashion.
To be worthy, not respectable, and
wealthy, not rich; to study hard,
think quietly, talk gently, act frankly;
to listen to stars and birds,
to babes and sages, with open heart;
to bear all cheerfully, do all bravely,
await occasions, hurry never.
In a word, to let the spiritual,
unbidden and unconscious, grow up
through the common.
  This will be my Symphony.

—WILLIAM HENRY CHANNING

I was not born to be forced. I will breathe after my
own fashion....If a plant cannot live according
to its nature, it dies; and so a man.

HENRY DAVID THOREAU

No one should ever make us do something that is
in conflict with our core nature, our identity, and
our personality.

Our job on earth is to learn more about our
own nature so we can flower and bloom in the
best possible light. How do you describe your
essential nature?

YOUR GRACE NOTES:

....
....
....

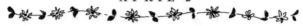

*B*ut not only medicine, engineering,
and painting are arts; living itself is an art.

ERICH FROMM

No one ever becomes an artist without a lot of
work and dedication to the truth and a serious
attempt to express that clarity beautifully. The art
of living requires the same honest principles.

The art of living is the highest of all callings. It
requires our undivided attention, commitment to
work in all areas of existence, so that we can
experience pleasure in the changing realities of
each precious moment.

YOUR GRACE NOTES:

....
....
....

The beginnings of all things are weak and tender.
We must therefore be clear-sighted in beginnings...

MICHEL DE MONTAIGNE

■ Often our enthusiasm is keener than our skills
at carrying out our goals. It is important that
what you begin be worthy of your full force.
Then jump in.

■ Don't tell anyone what you are starting to do. Your
strength comes from commitment. You will not
know the exact nature of the undertaking until you
set it in motion. Make something happen quietly.

YOUR GRACE NOTES:

■ ....
....
....
....
....

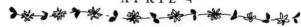

*L*earn to labor and wait.

HENRY WADSWORTH LONGFELLOW

■ Be a gardener of life. Lots of what you do doesn't show, like the roots of a tree. No work is ever wasted if it expresses something important to you.

■ It's best to send your ship out to sail first. Always do the groundwork before you come up for air and rest. This way the grass can grow while you do nothing. What work have you done that will bring your ship to shore?

YOUR GRACE NOTES:

■
....
....
....
....
....
....
....
....
....

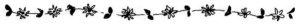

C hance governs all.
JOHN MILTON

⊠ The only possible continuity is of spirit, because everything is always in a state of dynamic transformation. That's the good news, because we are in the flow of this rejuvenescence all the time.

⊠ Welcome what chance provides. If it's good, seize it. Your doorbell may not ring twice.

YOUR GRACE NOTES:

⊠
....
....
....
....
....
....
....

God send you joy,
for sorrow will come fast enough.

JOHN CLARKE

■ We should live in a state of joy, of appreciation and love. Loss is hard when it is forever, so live in joy now, while it is possible.

■ Pretend you are living your life backward, starting on your deathbed. Write that script, because someday you'll be in that place. What feelings should you have now? How should you prepare yourself to have a life with few regrets?

YOUR GRACE NOTES:

■ ....
....
....

*I*t is impossible to live pleasurably without living
wisely, well, and justly, and impossible to live wisely,
well, and justly without living pleasurably.

EPICURUS

◼ Whenever you become tired of life, there
   is something wrong with you, not life. If
   "the process is the reality," and I believe
   Dr. Johnson was right, how can any of
   us afford to live a day unpleasantly
   when this is essentially all we can ever
   hope for before our time is up?

◼ Today, focus on pleasure. Pleasure in your
   relationships, pleasure in nature, pleasure in
   service, pleasure in self-expression, pleasure in
   the process. When you garden, take pleasure in
   digging in the soil. When you cook dinner, do it
   because you love to cook. Pleasure requires living
   in a state of pleasure.

YOUR GRACE NOTES:

◼   ....
    ....
    ....

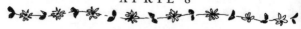

*When all at once I saw a crowd,
A host, of golden daffodils....*

WILLIAM WORDSWORTH

※ Whenever I see a daffodil, I think of Alexandra, three years old, in her first yellow Mary Janes and her yellow bonnet. How utterly beautiful and fragile life is!

※ Spring and daffodils gently urge us to love life and appreciate its mysteries.

YOUR GRACE NOTES:

※

....
....
....
....
....
....
....
....
....

*R*eflect that life is composed of
small incidents and petty occurrences....

SAMUEL JOHNSON

◫ There are no big events in life that aren't the
result of a great many small happenings.

◫ Every single small thing you do builds and
attaches itself to a bigger whole. By paying
careful attention to each act we perform we are
living in a loving manner.

YOUR GRACE NOTES:

◫
....
....
....
....
....
....
....
....

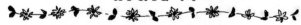

*P*ure logic is the ruin of the spirit.
ANTOINE DE SAINT-EXUPÉRY

■ Energy increases with happiness. Creativity requires serendipity and a playful, receptive spirit. Let yourself go when you are trying to invent something new.

■ To revitalize yourself change your routines. Have breakfast in the garden. Or take your newspaper to the local coffee shop. Isn't that where you'd rather be?

YOUR GRACE NOTES:

■ ....
....
....

*S*cenery is fine,
but human nature is finer.

JOHN KEATS

- Sometimes I like to talk to the trees but I'd prefer to talk to you. I like learning what you're thinking about and what you're feeling.

- Let's go for a walk together so we can become invigorated by each other and the beauty around us.

YOUR GRACE NOTES:

....
....
....
....
....
....
....

Time is not a line,
but a series of now-points.

TAISEN DESHIMAM

⊠ Time is made up of little dots. Tick. Tick. Tick. It's what we do when we're able to connect the series of now-points that will represent us when time is no longer ours to use.

⊠ One of the reasons gardening is so much fun is because we become one with the earth. What do you love to do when you are in the nowness of time?

YOUR GRACE NOTES:

⊠

....
....
....
....

*O*ne to-day is worth two to-morrows.
BENJAMIN FRANKLIN

Let's not take a chance. Let's live all our days to
the hilt. Here's to today. Celebrate it and christen
it beautifully.

When I was younger I longed for Friday night.
But now I love each day equally because every
day offers us the same time. Isn't time our
opportunity? *Now* is the best time.

YOUR GRACE NOTES:

....
....
....
....
....
....

*N*ature does nothing uselessly.

ARISTOTLE

▣ There is a plan. We are in it. We are in it together. Nature reminds us that there is an order to beauty. There is a reason for everything.

▣ Nature doesn't waste time. Avoid the redundant, the mindless attention to a presumed duty, the dreary false starts. Focus on the true reasons you do what you do. Are there things you can drop because they aren't vital to you and therefore won't survive? Nature reminds us that rootless things die.

YOUR GRACE NOTES:

▣ ....
....
....

...*Arrange to live sensibly, truthfully and always
with a sense of our own limitations....true peace of
mind comes from accepting the worst.*

LIN YUTANG

■ When we overdo, we're out of control. Overload
results in chaos and even sickness. Limit yourself
so you can enjoy some peace of mind.

■ Is your life in balance? Are you working too hard?
Do you have too many challenges? Do you have
enough fun? Minor readjustments will make you
feel whole again. I just had a nap. Wow, what a
difference!

YOUR GRACE NOTES:

■ ....
....
....
....

*C*olors speak all languages.

JOSEPH ADDISON

▣ I understand a great deal about the energy, attitude and spirit of people because of the colors they surround themselves with. We reveal so much, even in our silence.

▣ What are your favorite colors of Springtime? What colors do you like in your garden? Do you enjoy wearing the same colors? Study the colors in bloom in the days ahead and you will learn how they affect you.

YOUR GRACE NOTES:

▣ ....
....
....
....
....
....

Love everybody you love;
you can never tell when they might not be there.

NANCY BUSH ELLIS

▨ Keep your relationships up to date. After someone
dies it is harder to express your love.

▨ Out of the blue, send a love note to someone
you're thinking about today. You'll never
understand fully how much it could mean to the
recipient. You'll feel divinely connected.

YOUR GRACE NOTES:

▨
....
....
....
....
....
....

Trifles make perfection —
and perfection is no trifle.

MICHELANGELO

■ When we care about the
smallest veining in a slab of
marble, or the grain of a
piece of wood, we are aware
that everything is alive and
everything is significant.

■ The smallest detail, when cared for lovingly, can
turn out to be a masterpiece. Whether you are
working on your yard or whipping up a salad for
lunch, you are doing something meaningful when
you do your best.

YOUR GRACE NOTES:

■

....

....

....

....

....

....

....

*L*ife teaches us to be less harsh
with ourselves and with others.

LIN YUTANG

We need all the nurturing, loving kindness that life
can offer as we face the inevitable difficulties and
struggles. I've learned to treat myself gently
because, with a few exceptions, I'm doing my best.

We have no right to judge others. Our job is to
look at ourselves. Never feel guilty when you are
caring for yourself. Who else can take care of your
physical, emotional and spiritual needs better?
Who else really knows what's appropriate? Today,
let go of guilt when you do things for yourself.
This is your job. Consider it maintenance! Our
well-being depends on this simple truth.

YOUR GRACE NOTES:

....
....
....

*C*ultivate peace and harmony with all....
GEORGE WASHINGTON

🔲 Whenever I feel angry or frustrated toward
anyone it poisons my spirit. Discord toward others
hurts us and does no earthly good.

🔲 The world needs all of us to participate positively
and productively in trying to make a better life for
everyone. Think of large issues; avoid petty,
useless stuff.

YOUR GRACE NOTES:

🔲
....
....
....
....
....
....

You can never plan the future by the past.

EDMUND BURKE

■ Don't assume anything. The past is dead. The future is right now, this moment.

■ The way to look ahead is to examine your present circumstances. Think about your life five years ago. Your situation is different now. Stay current and say good-bye to the past. It's over.

YOUR GRACE NOTES:

■
....
....
....
....
....
....
....
....

*A*ll are needed by each one:
Nothing is fair or good alone.

RALPH WALDO EMERSON

🔳 We are interdependent and this adds great depth
to our lives.

🔳 Today, focus on all the contributions others have
made and continue to make in shaping your life.
All of us work as a team, helping where we can,
lending support and encouragement in our own
way. Here's a salute to our needing and
appreciating one another.

YOUR GRACE NOTES:

🔳
....
....
....

*V*ision is the art of seeing things invisible.
JONATHAN SWIFT

🔳 We can carry the world inside us once we accept
the mysteries we can't see.

🔳 Train yourself to become more visual. Imagine
how something will look. With practice you will be
able to envision anything.

YOUR GRACE NOTES:

🔳 ....
....
....
....
....
....
....
....

*T*he quieter you become,
the more you can hear.

BABA RAM DASS

■ Until we calm down and become still, we won't be able to hear ourselves. Listening requires silence and our being still.

■ Pay attention to the noises around you. The chime of the hall clock, the birds singing. A child laughing. The coffeemaker snoring, the gurgle of the soup kettle, the flag flapping in modulating waves of sound like the flames of a fire. But be most attentive to the sound of your voice, what you say to yourself as well as what you utter.

YOUR GRACE NOTES:

■ ....
   ....
   ....

*K*now how sublime a thing it is
To suffer and be strong.

HENRY WADSWORTH LONGFELLOW

■ Be in touch with your pain. It is an important part of who you are.

■ Don't be hard on yourself. And don't be embarassed by your pain. Go through it with dignity. It will enhance you.

YOUR GRACE NOTES:

■
....
....
....
....
....
....
....
....

*P*leasure is nothing else
but the intermission of pain.

JOHN SELDEN

Pleasure is the gift of grace. We can't take it for granted. We can wish for it but we can't control it. All the more reason to embrace it fully when it is there.

Accept that half your life will be pain, your own or that of loved ones. Look around at all the suffering. Look around at all the joy.

YOUR GRACE NOTES:

....
....
....

*for a life of sensations
rather than of thoughts.*

JOHN KEATS

- When we feel and sense something intuitively,
  these emotions can be powerfully beautiful. Let
  them flow through you and don't ruin the aura by
  thinking about it. Let it happen.

- Everything can't be understood or analyzed.
  When I am in an open mood and my state of mind
  is receptive, I shun thought deliberately . Trust the
  muse. Just being in that state is more than enough.

YOUR GRACE NOTES:

....
....
....
....
....

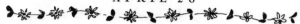

There is but one unconditional commandment....
to bring about the very largest total universe
of good which we can see.

WILLIAM JAMES

🔲 It certainly makes life worthwhile when you
can think about doing good and give back to
the world.

🔲 Having a purpose, reaching out beyond yourself,
being outgoing, is revitalizing to the giver. Every
good deed you do genuinely comes back to you in
abundance, even when no one directly thanks you.
It's felt in your soul.

YOUR GRACE NOTES:

🔲 ....
....
....

*O*pinion is ultimately determined by the feelings,
and not by the intellect.

HERBERT SPENCER

■ My information comes to me through my gut. I
listen to and revere my intuition. When I don't, I
get myself in trouble. We don't always decide by
our intellect but often through feelings rooted in
experience.

■ Consider your opinions. Were they formed by
intellect or logic? Or were they influenced by
your intuition and emotional experience? You *can*
determine the basis of your judgments. Go on a
bike ride and muse over these thoughts.

YOUR GRACE NOTES:

■ ....
....
....
....

Be of good cheer....
HOMER

- A cheerful disposition is luminous. It illuminates everyone and everything. Being grumpy has no rewards. Be of good cheer.

- Being cheerful is an attitude. We all choose our moods. We can be glad, giving thanks for all our blessings or we can focus in on ourselves and be down and gloomy. Today when you're alone, monitor your disposition. If it rains, you have the power to spread sunshine. Use it.

YOUR GRACE NOTES:

....
....
....
....
....

*L*et all thy joys be as the month of May....

FRANCIS QUARLES

◪ April supplied us with enough rain to nourish our garden and now we have May to renew our spirits. Use the entire month to focus on all the joys in your life.

◪ Hang a tiny basket of flowers on the door handle of your child's room today as a symbol of the merry month of May. Or tie a plaid taffeta ribbon on the handle. If you have a daughter, she can wear the ribbon in her hair.

YOUR GRACE NOTES:

◪ ....
....
....

*For each ecstatic instant
We must an anguish pay
In keen and quivering ratio
To the ecstasy.*

EMILY DICKINSON

▦ The deeper our capacity for joy, the more we will feel pain when it happens. Accept the other side of *your* coin.

▦ You can never love too much, care too much, or be too vulnerable. Be grateful for who you are.

YOUR GRACE NOTES:

▦ ....
....
....
....
....

*B*ehind seeming permanence lies constant flux.

HERACLITUS

▣ You are changing and everyone around you is changing. The rate of change differs; accept that.

▣ Don't feel guilty when you outgrow a love or a friendship. New ones will take their place for both of you. Wow!

YOUR GRACE NOTES:

▣ ....
....
....
....
....
....
....

*T*here is not a sprig of grass that shoots
uninteresting to me.

THOMAS JEFFERSON

   Bring your full self to everything you observe and
feel. Everything that surrounds you offers itself to
you. Take it.

   What interests you? Make a list. Make it long.

YOUR GRACE NOTES:

   ....
   ....
   ....
   ....
   ....
   ....

> *Great emergencies and crises show us
> how much greater our vital resources
> are than we had supposed.*
>
> WILLIAM JAMES

■ You will never be asked to bear more than you
can cope with. Crises tap into a strength that you
didn't know was there. Be proud of this surge of
inner strength, and be grateful.

■ Remember that in spite of the courage you
summon you may still feel need. You *must* reach
out for support.

YOUR GRACE NOTES:

■ ....
....
....

*G*ive yourself no unnecessary pain.
PERCY BYSSHE SHELLEY

■ When it happens it's real, and you'll know it. A loved one dies. You've lost your job. You've lost a friend. You've lost your health. Grieve only when you are in pain; don't anticipate it.

■ There's an Italian saying that urges you not to bandage your head before you've broken it. So don't.

YOUR GRACE NOTES:

■ ....
....
....
....
....

*W*hat gives life its value you can find — and lose. But never possess. This holds good above all for the Truth about Life.

DAG HAMMARSKJÖLD

■ We are here as visitors, tourists. We can appreciate what we experience but we can't possess anything, any more than we can stay here forever.

■ We live life in little moments that are soon gone. Each day holds possibilities for great discoveries and hidden joys. Enjoy each small amusement. The only thing you can grasp hold of is the moment, now.

YOUR GRACE NOTES:

■ ....
....
....
....

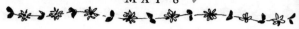

The most visible joy can only reveal itself to us
when we've transformed it, within.

RAINER MARIA RILKE

🔲 Whenever you experience awesome beauty,
absorb it inside yourself. It does affect your soul.
Once there, it lifts your spirits and is alive in you
now and as a memory. Beauty unappreciated is
beauty unknown.

🔲 How many gardens have you seen, over your
lifetime, that you remember? What's amazing is
that we remember where, when, who we were
with. I remember what I was wearing when I *really*
saw my mother's garden for the first time. I was
three. These impressions are our best inheritance
and pay us the greatest dividends.

YOUR GRACE NOTES:

🔲 ....
....
....

*L*ive your life in a manner that never infringes
on the happiness of anyone.

EKNATH EASWARAN

▣ No one can truly be happy if this happiness has
come at someone else's expense.

▣ Everyone is us; we are all in this together. We will
be more understanding of the needs of others
when we are able to care for our own.

YOUR GRACE NOTES:

▣ ....
....
....
....
....
....
....
....

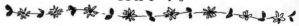

We are the children of our landscape; it dictates
behavior and even thought in the measure
to which we are responsive to it.

LAWRENCE DURRELL

⬚ One of the saddest things about poverty —
particularly urban poverty — is that children
grow up surrounded by graffiti and garbage.
All of us should have memories of years of natural
beauty to draw from as a resource whenever we
need them to feed our work and our life.

⬚ Go on a walk with a child. Chances are you will
hear all about nature and the times you went to the
lake, or the beach or the mountains. Nature is a
loving companion and for this we are blessed.

YOUR GRACE NOTES:

⬚ ....
   ....
   ....

What is natural is never disgraceful.

EURIPIDES

⊞ Nature teaches us that beauty doesn't have
straight lines and everything
bends and moves in graceful
ways. When we act naturally
we are never awkward nor do
we make fools of ourselves.

⊞ Look around you. Are there some things that seem
right because they've been there for a long time?
An old stone wall that's been there since the
eighteenth century, for example, is natural. Admire
all that is authentic in yourself and your immediate
surroundings.

YOUR GRACE NOTES:

⊞ ....
....
....
....
....
....
....

*P*leasure is very seldom found where it is sought.

SAMUEL JOHNSON

🪷 We don't have a great deal of fun when we're pleasure-bent. Like joy, pleasure is a by-product. While we're fully engaged in something useful or good we're often given a bonus.

🪷 Our enjoyment and gratification most often come because of some effort we've made. In working we are able to create something that wouldn't have been there without our effort. What are some of the things you've done recently that gave you (and others) pleasure?

YOUR GRACE NOTES:

🪷 ....
....
....

In life as well as in art, Zen never wastes energy
in stopping to explain; it only indicates.

ALAN WATTS

When we mature spiritually we are
less interested in didactic preaching.
We learn best by inference and
illusion. We draw our own
conclusions and therefore own
the information as our truth.

Be a mentor to someone younger who admires
you. There are a dozen people I've looked up to in
my lifetime and many of them have become
mentors. But never once have any of these wise
men and women told me what to think. They
merely loved me, believed in me, cared about what
I thought and felt, and by their presence, revealed
important truths to me.

YOUR GRACE NOTES:

....
....

*N*ature never did betray the heart that loved her.
WILLIAM WORDSWORTH

🔲 From any effort I expend to plant and grow
something, I always reap rewards greater than
the labor I extend. Mother Nature teaches us how
to love.

🔲 What have you planted in your garden that will
bloom and ripen in the weeks and months ahead?
Just think of the bounty as a miracle. The
more we expose ourselves to all these magical
happenings the more we revere life.

YOUR GRACE NOTES:

🔲 ....
....
....

*M*easure your health by your sympathy
with morning and Spring.
HENRY DAVID THOREAU

■ We are given dazzling sunlight, fragrant air, new
birth, beauty all around us and we have to register
it all in our soul. While we are experiencing
morning and Spring, somewhere in the world
there is darkness and sadness. That's life.

■ Peter always says we should put these joyous days
in our emotional bank, saving them up for the
inevitable stormy days in the future. Write down
how you feel today. Write a poem,
take a picture, sing a song.
Arrange a bouquet of flowers.
Do a watercolor. Express your
sense of joy in your own way.
You can make this moment last.

YOUR GRACE NOTES:

■ ....
....
....

*P*ray you, love, remember:
and there is pansies, that's for thoughts.

WILLIAM SHAKESPEARE

■ Pansies have such sweet faces. I'll never forget
seeing window boxes some twenty years ago
brimming with pansies against velvet morning-blue
shutters on a white clapboard New England house.

■ Put a small bunch of pansies in a glass tumbler and
place them by a child's bed.

■ Buy a few packets of pansy seeds and send them
to someone you love.

YOUR GRACE NOTES:

■ ....
....
....

*T*ask not for a larger garden,
But for finer seeds.

RUSSELL HERMA CORNWELL

■ We don't need to be greedy when it comes to our garden. We want one that is manageable. The whole idea of a garden is so you can *be* a gardener. A garden is not a chore for others to handle.

■ Plant your own seeds, even if it is only in a window box. Get nice and dirty. Let's all do a bit of gardening. I have several pots in need of planting. What will you do? It's Rose Marie's birthday; let's cut some flowers and make a bouquet for her.

YOUR GRACE NOTES:

■ ....
....
....

157

I've taken my fun where I've found it.

RUDYARD KIPLING

▣ I married Peter on this fine day in May and carried lilies of the valley. I've lived in a state of appreciation and joy ever since. Let's celebrate today. Why not?

▣ It's lilac time. The buds are about to burst and my spirits are soaring. As a child we had lilacs hugging our sleeping porch in Connecticut and I'm intoxicated by the smell and memories.

YOUR GRACE NOTES:

▣ ....
....
....
....
....

*T*ake the gentle path.
GEORGE HERBERT

■ We choose our own path and then we reach a point of no return. A peaceful, serene, tender life bears fruit.

■ We can't have everything but we can point ourselves in the right direction. Be willing to resist anything that takes you off your chosen path.

YOUR GRACE NOTES:

■ ....
....
....
....
....
....
....

Love is exactly as strong as life.

JOSEPH CAMPBELL

▣ The more we love life the more love we have to share. Loving life increases our energy and passions.

▣ What are you most enthusiastic about today? Have you given yourself enough time to work on your project? Do. It's more important than sleep.

YOUR GRACE NOTES:

▣ ....
....
....
....
....
....
....

The joy of life is to put out one's power in
some natural and useful or harmless way.

OLIVER WENDELL HOLMES

☒ Everything we do requires us to reveal our
inner longings. Identify them clearly and make
productive use of them.

☒ The wise people who accomplish much in their
lifetime know the secret of happiness, which is to
act out one's own interior stirrings and make them
concrete. There is no greater joy than to find and
bring forth personal truths.

YOUR GRACE NOTES:

☒ ....
....
....

A wise man sees as much as he ought,
not as much as he can.

MICHEL DE MONTAIGNE

■ Concentrate on seeing all the beauty your soul can absorb but turn away from what is ugly and vile and degrading. The higher your sights, the better your spirits.

■ We all have neighbors. Greet them on the sidewalk or in the elevator, but try not to peer through their windows. Windows are to look out from, not into.

YOUR GRACE NOTES:

■ ....
....
....
....

*Mu*sic produces a kind of pleasure which human
nature cannot do without.

CONFUCIUS

■ This time of year I most enjoy the concert of birds
singing at the tops of their tiny lungs. There's time
for the band on the Fourth of July.

■ I'm enjoying *Watermark*, by Enya, a tape given to
me by my daughter Alexandra, and *Shadows*, by the
piano player Danny Wright, which was a gift from
a friend. What are you listening to right now? Cat
Stevens?

YOUR GRACE NOTES:

■ ....
....
....
....

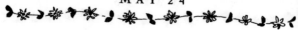

*R*ight now a moment of time is fleeting by!
....We must become that moment....forgetting
everything that has been seen before our time.

PAUL CÉZANNE

🔲 Artists show us how we can interpret the world
afresh. Our insights are vital to feed the moment.

🔲 Forget everything that you have ever felt or
thought before. You have a clean slate. You can't
remember pain. Now is the time to get inside the
moment and let it illuminate, enlighten and lead
you to greater joy and appreciation.

YOUR GRACE NOTES:

🔲 ....
....
....

We shall all be as good as dead one day, but in the interests of life we should postpone this moment as long as possible, and this we can only do by never allowing our picture of the world to become rigid.

CARL JUNG

■ We'll be rigid in the old pine box, but for now we have to respond to life in a lively way with an open mind. If I've learned anything over the years, it is to listen and not to be controlling.

■ Everyone should be free to change his mind. Peter never liked tinted glass. I came home with some wonderful glasses with polka dots in fun colors and I served him a drink. He just held the glass in bemusement; after taking a sip he said, "I like this funky glass. Tell me about it."

YOUR GRACE NOTES:

■ ....
....
....

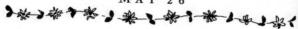

*T*he proper use of imagination is to give beauty to the world…the gift of imagination is used to cast over the commonplace workaday world a veil of beauty and make it throb with our esthetic enjoyment.

LIN YUTANG

⊠ Imagine what a dull world we'd live in if we couldn't envision the invisible and couldn't put a few fanciful touches and twists to reality. Beauty is in the eye of the beholder and we are as happy as we wish to be.

⊠ Pretend you have a camera with you and, as you go about your day, look and really see what is around you. As an interior designer, I'm paid to imagine. See what you can improve, everywhere, with the mystical, marvelous use of your imagination.

YOUR GRACE NOTES:

⊠ ....
....
....

*M*anners speak the idiom of their soil.

THOMAS GRAY

▣ The more down-to-earth we are, the more genuine and sincere, the more relaxed we become and can let go of our pretensions.

▣ Think about some of the small pretensions you have become prone to. Sometimes I hear an artificial accent and I think it was bought in a charm school. To be yourself is a gift. If you are genuine, your manners will reflect that.

YOUR GRACE NOTES:

▣ ....
....
....
....
....

MAY 28

Patience is the best remedy for every trouble.
TITUS MACCIUS PLAUTUS

■ When we're in trouble, dwelling on it doesn't really help. We can feel sad, we can grieve, but eventually we have to move on. Time does heal, and when you are going through a difficult patch, remember, you don't want to make it any worse. Act constructively.

■ In times of trouble, think about what's useful. Stay with it and work things out. Endurance, perseverance, tenacity and persistence come to mind. My favorite childhood book was *The Little Engine That Could*. I think I can. I think I can. I think I can. I thought I could. I thought I could.

YOUR GRACE NOTES:

■ ....
....
....

The shortest mistakes are always the best.
MOLIÈRE

■ If you feel uncomfortable with anything, you should reconsider your situation. Cut your losses. Far better to admit a mistake than to persist in it and allow it to develop into a nightmare.

■ What mistakes have you made recently? I make a lot of mistakes but I'm learning to take responsibility for them and accept that I'm wrong. It's a whole lot better all around. What's wrong? Fix it.

YOUR GRACE NOTES:

■ ....
....
....

Sorrow makes us wise.

ALFRED, LORD TENNYSON

■ Until you've gone through an experience it is hard to speak convincingly of it to someone else. That's why we can be helpful to others when we know firsthand something painful. Even sorrow over a loss can be beautiful because it brings us in close touch with how much we care.

■ We're able to reevaluate what's *really* important when we experience loss. From that comes growth and true appreciation.

YOUR GRACE NOTES:

■ ....
....
....
....
....

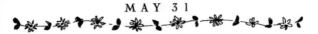

Go in peace.

ABRAHAM LINCOLN

■ Peace be with us all. What a wonderful way to
live, to experience harmony and order and live in
an agreeable, calm atmosphere. This is the way life
should be. Always.

■ How peaceful do you feel right now? When the
fax paper gets stuck and the sink stops up and
the phone won't stop ringing, I go for a bike ride.
Find some peace. Our nerves, our home and our
country crave peace.

YOUR GRACE NOTES:

■ ....
....
....

I find that I have painted my life — things happening in my life — without knowing.

GEORGIA O'KEEFFE

🔲 We express our life through our work and our interests. Our lives are snapshots, lived moment by moment and who we are becomes clearer through what we create.

🔲 How do you express yourself? If you have to be known for only one contribution, what would you say it is? Eventually we all have to define ourselves and then get going.

YOUR GRACE NOTES:

🔲 ....
....
....

No duty is more urgent than
that of returning thanks.

SAINT AMBROSE

■ Whenever we thank someone, we become bigger
people. When we acknowledge to another person
that he or she has made a difference, we are
showing appreciation. Be in a continuous state
of thanksgiving.

■ You can never express thanks
too often. A charming, poised
and outgoing woman from
Birmingham, Alabama, Mrs. Blount,
shared a secret with me several years
ago. "Whenever you think of the contribution
someone has made to you in the past — a
schoolteacher or the person performing your
marriage ceremony — write a letter and thank
them. I call this the second thank you."

YOUR GRACE NOTES:

■ ....
....
....

173

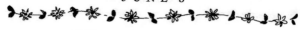

We must cultivate our garden.

VOLTAIRE

▦ Alone, we can't change the universe but we can
nurture and nourish those near us. When we do
all we can and bring forth our best, we are doing
our share to make the world a more humane place.

▦ What are you doing this month to improve, elevate
and develop yourself? We can't help others unless
we have something useful to give. Redefine what it
is you want to do and then make a plan to train
toward that goal.

YOUR GRACE NOTES:

▦ ....
....
....

*R*ivers are roads that move.

BLAISE PASCAL

■ Nothing is ever the same. Rivers are symbolic of our lives, moving and ever-changing.

■ Movement is life. We feel freedom as we move with the currents. No power please.

YOUR GRACE NOTES:

■ ....
....
....
....
....
....
....
....
....
....
....

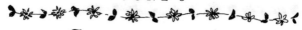

...Inaction saps the vigor of the mind.
LEONARDO DA VINCI

■ Nothing makes one more tired than just sitting around purposelessly. That's quite different from sitting in solitude when we can daydream in peace and then spring into action. Our minds need to be occupied not to feel sluggish.

■ Often unrelated actions or thoughts trigger concentration. Something kicks in, like an energy charge. The mind is an amazing electrical appliance. Plug it in and it goes.

YOUR GRACE NOTES:

■ ....
....
....
....
....
....

The more he gives to others,
the more he possesses of his own.

LAO-TZU

▨ As a child I never understood what my parents
meant when they said "It's better to give than to
receive." I now know that when we give to
others we do this out of abundance. We have
already received and therefore we can give.

▨ We can't give away something we don't already
have. Where does it come from? Give all you can
whenever the spirit moves you because it is a sign
that you have a fertile spirit, which replenishes
itself through giving.

YOUR GRACE NOTES:

▨ ....
....
....

I hear the trumpets of the morning blowing.

HENRY WADSWORTH LONGFELLOW

🔲 Poets remind us that there are trumpets of the morning. When you wake up, be a poet and hear the sounds of celebration.

🔲 Wake up an hour earlier than anyone else in your house so you can have an hour of reverie. Daydream, muse, fantasize, meditate. The trumpets of the morning will blow; be awake to hear them.

YOUR GRACE NOTES:

🔲 ....
....
....
....
....
....

*W*hy stay we on the earth except to grow?

ROBERT BROWNING

▓ If we can't increase our skills, expand our knowledge and enlarge our soul, what is the point of growing old?

▓ After we finish growing physically we are not grown up. Now we should focus on interior growth to expand awareness, sensitivity, and love. Let's grow up together.

YOUR GRACE NOTES:

▓ ....
....
....
....
....
....
....

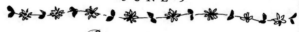

Beauty is the gift of God.

ARISTOTLE

■ Beauty is not automatic. It is a gift. We can try to live beautifully, doing everything as attractively and lovingly as possible, but ultimately we look to nature and our creator for our inspiration.

■ What's beautiful in your life right now? What plans do you have to create something beautiful? Our neighbor planted an apple tree in her front yard after her daughter was born.

YOUR GRACE NOTES:

■ ....
....
....
....
....

I loaf and invite my soul.
WALT WHITMAN

■ Sometimes we have to give our mind a rest. Whenever I put my feet up, lean back in a chair and gaze at the sky, thoughts flash around in a playful way.

■ A serious gardener, after working herself into an amazing sweat by pruning, digging, planting and cutting, Sally gets a cool drink, goes down to her hammock by the pond and has a rest. When's the last time you had a serious loaf?

YOUR GRACE NOTES:

■ ....
....
....
....

...It is the first part of intelligence to recognize our precarious estate in life, and the first part of courage to be not at all abashed before the fact.

ROBERT LOUIS STEVENSON

■ I used to worry a lot. Life seemed dangerous and scary. But now I feel that it is a challenging, exciting journey and the surprises are a part of the thrill of the unknown. We all are in this together and can help one another to be brave.

■ E. B. White's wife, Katherine, planted flowers in her garden when she was dying, knowing she wouldn't see them. All of us are aware how vulnerable we are in our relationships and in our health. Increase your strength and heighten your skills. Now won't always be the same.

YOUR GRACE NOTES:

■ ....
....
....

*A*h, but in such matters
it is only the first step that is difficult.
MADAME DU DEFFAND

- Perfectionists have the hardest time with beginnings because they're waiting for the perfect moment, which never comes. Hours, days, weeks and years slip by. Realize that the best time is when you take that first step. Take courage.

- The first step has already been taken because you have gathered information and materials. Kandinsky didn't like to face a blank canvas so he put a little dot on the top and then relaxed and began to paint. Where are you going to put your symbolic dot today and take that first step?

YOUR GRACE NOTES:

....
....
....

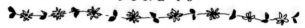

*N*othing is there to come, and nothing past.
But an eternal now does always last.

ABRAHAM CROWLEY

■ I have a fascination with now. Everything is alive
and real to me as I live it. Now affects the nows
that follow, so when we get now right,
everything has a chance of falling into place.

■ We don't remember ordinary occurrences. What
we remember are the touching, moving, joyful
moments. Virginia Woolf wrote about "moments
big as years." Now, what are you going to do to
make of this moment an eternal *now*?

YOUR GRACE NOTES:

■ ....
....
....
....

It is the addition of strangeness to beauty
that constitutes the romantic character of art.

WALTER PATER

- We are drawn to the unfamiliar, the unusual, the new and unknown aspects of beauty and art.

- Strangeness is not a pejorative word but is merely unfamiliar. One of the things that appeals most to us is to experience an artist's novel point of view. Matisse certainly showed us about color and form.

YOUR GRACE NOTES:

....
....
....
....
....
....

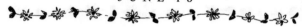

I'd like to go climbing a birch tree....

ROBERT FROST

🔲 Birch trees have always been a favorite. I love the white bark and their graceful height and yielding qualities. What is your favorite tree?

🔲 Hiking through a birch forest with someone you love is amazing grace. Have you ever tasted birch beer? I put birch logs in our fireplace in summer to make it look more alive. Do you like to climb ˙ birch trees too?

YOUR GRACE NOTES:

🔲 ....
....
....
....
....

JUNE 16

The first beginnings of things
cannot be distinguished by the eye.

JULIUS CAESAR

▨ We have to have faith in life because we will never be able to see everything that is affecting us. Believe in the intangible, unseeable phenomena in life.

▨ The eye is not the only way of seeing. We can experience situations and events in different ways. Planning your vegetable garden is exciting because when the time is right, you will see juicy, plump, ripe, red tomatoes. Baskets full of them. Plan now for what you can't see. When you see it, it's often too late.

YOUR GRACE NOTES:

▨ ....
....
....

*P*atience is the companion of wisdom.

AUGUSTINE

■ Anything valuable is going to take time. Be patient and tolerant with yourself and others. Do your best and let go.

■ What are you waiting for? Nature reminds us that we must wait to harvest. Waiting for something you care deeply about isn't the worst thing in the world. You have to have something to look forward to.

YOUR GRACE NOTES:

■ ....
....
....
....

The time of the singing of birds is come....
SONG OF SOLOMON

- Romance is in the air, and "the voice of the turtle dove is heard in the land." Rejoice. Share in the wonder of love, hope and youth.

- When the time is ripe, make a commitment. Make a vow and make a promise to love and be obedient to your covenant. What's your resolve? Write it down and live it.

YOUR GRACE NOTES:

- ....
....
....
....
....
....
....

*N*ature permits the best part of the picture; carves the
best part of the statue; builds the best part of the
house; and speaks the best part of the oration.

RALPH WALDO EMERSON

It's all here for us to tap into and work with the
elements we have now. What you are essentially is
all you'll ever become. Tap into nature and your
human nature for clues and answers.

Meditate in your own way. Go for a walk in the
woods with your dog. Go to the beach. Sit in a
chair and shut your eyes. Sit on the floor in a lotus
position and look at a flower. Light a candle. Think
about nature and love.

YOUR GRACE NOTES:

....
....
....

But the tender grace of a day that is dead will never come back to me.

ALFRED, LORD TENNYSON

- Every morning when you wake up you have the opportunity to experience tender grace. Yesterday will never come again but you have today. A friend calls today to-now. Now. You have everything. Call your godmother or someone close.

- What are you going to do that will bring grace, order and beauty to your day? Begin a new project. Gather the books you intend to read this summer. Read as many good books as you can from your child's high school reading list. Consider reading them together.

YOUR GRACE NOTES:

- ....
....
....

...*Perform* every act in life
as though it were your last.
MARCUS AURELIUS

■ My best friend died of cancer when she was in
her early forties. The day she died, she rode an
elephant with her daughter in Marrakesh. When
I came back from the funeral there was a postcard
telling me about her great vacation. Live with
this vitality.

■ Your family is as sacred as any guests who come
for a visit. Do everything to bring elegance, order,
beauty and joy into each task you perform. This
morning, set the breakfast table as if you were
having company. Make it really special.

YOUR GRACE NOTES:

■ ....
....
....

*Talk of mysteries! Think of our life in nature —
daily to be shown matter, to come in contact with it —
rocks, trees, wind on our cheeks! the solid earth!
the actual world! the common sense! Contact! Contact!
Who are we? Where are we?*

LIN YUTANG

Plan to spend a night under the
stars. Why is it that we talk to
ourselves more honestly when we are
surrounded by sky, grass, trees and a
pond? Women, take off your high heels and
fingernail polish. It doesn't work here.

Today, instead of meeting a friend for a walk,
go by yourself. Have a really good conversation.
Ask yourself questions the way Lin Yutang did.
"*Who* are we? *Where* are we?" Wonderful fun.
Don't bring a Walkman. Just walk and talk.

YOUR GRACE NOTES:

....
....
....

*T*he pleasure of love is in loving. We are happier
in the passion we feel than in that we arouse.

DUC DE LA ROCHEFOUCAULD

🔲 I love loving others. To love someone is its own
reward. How you feel about the love process is the
key. Just keep loving and fuel that passion.

🔲 Who are the people you really love? Say their
names out loud. Love, feel loving, act kindly and
compassionately toward others. You'll always be
enriched. Don't measure love. It's all right to love
someone more than they love you. You may have
a larger capacity to love than others.

YOUR GRACE NOTES:

🔲 ....
....
....

*U*se no hurtful deceit; think innocently and justly
and, if you speak, speak accordingly.
BENJAMIN FRANKLIN

■ There are consequences to our actions. Go about
life's journey. If we think beautiful thoughts, and
act unmaliciously, if we care about what we do,
how we act and what we say, we will be rewarded
in hidden moments.

■ Be open. Honesty is good for your health. Being
able to live with yourself is more important than
anything else. When you speak, do it in a manner
that dignifies you and makes you feel whole inside.

YOUR GRACE NOTES:

■ ....
....
....

*From the senses come all trustworthiness,
all good conscience, all evidence of truth.*

FRIEDRICH NIETZSCHE

■ Trust your gut. Remember that your sixth sense is intuition.

■ Work on developing all your senses, fine-tune them so you may appreciate everything more acutely, and see everything with greater clarity. Rate your success from 1 to 10. Know that your life depends on improving your awareness.

YOUR GRACE NOTES:

■ ....
....
....
....
....
....

The story's about you.

HORACE

■ All of us write our own autobiography. We just do it in our own way. How are you going to tell and record *your* story?

■ If you don't keep a journal, start now. Write down the things that interest you. Write in detail. Journals are revealing.

YOUR GRACE NOTES:

■ ....
....
....
....
....
....
....
....
....

O mortal man, think mortal thoughts!
EURIPIDES

▦ It never appealed to me to save up living for the next life. Live now, live in the nowness of time and when death comes you will be ready.

▦ Enjoy the physical aspects of your day. The sensuous feeling of a shower after a rigorous workout. The touch of a dog's ear. The taste of an herb omelet. Feel it immortally.

YOUR GRACE NOTES:

▦ ....
....
....
....
....
....

*C*an we ever have too much of a good thing?

MIGUEL DE CERVANTES

I love food. I look forward to every meal. If you have a healthy attitude you will have a healthy appetite. Never say the word *diet* again. Why ruin a pleasure? Eating is fun.

Your enjoyment of food can be enhanced by the atmosphere, the company, the presentation and selection. Studies show that the appearance of a meal helps iron to be absorbed into the body, for example. One of the reasons people develop eating disorders is because they equate food with love. Food is not love. Don't use food as a compensation for what is missing in your life.

YOUR GRACE NOTES:

....
....
....
....
....

We are lovers of beauty without extravagance,
and lovers of wisdom...

THUCYDIDES

◼ The older I get the more I like simple, honest
things. Think about your clothes. Think about
your furniture and decorations. Do they suit your
personality? Do they reflect the real you?

◼ Remember the triangle of simplicity,
appropriateness and beauty, and live by it today.
Tonight bring a basket to the beach, throw down
a blanket, and have a picnic with the children.
I intend to.

YOUR GRACE NOTES:

◼ ....
....
....

*T*he bravest are the tenderest —
The loving are the daring.

BAYARD TAYLOR

■ Reaching out to others, being outgoing — being
kind, gentle and thoughtful — these qualities
require great sensitivity and daring. The more we
forget about our own ego, the more open we are
to love.

■ Do you "double dare" me to love you? Remember
that childhood game? If you love you will be
content. Tomorrow we move into a new season,
summer. As we walk along a sandy beach with all
its freedom, let's love ourselves and each other.

YOUR GRACE NOTES:

■ ....
....
....

$\mathscr{S}$UMMER

❖

Know thyself.

INSCRIPTION ON THE TEMPLE
TO APOLLO AT DELPHI

The good life is not only good for one's conscience; it is good for art, good for knowledge, good for health, good for fellowship.

— LEWIS MUMFORD

JULY 1

Did you know that secret?
The awful thing is that beauty is mysterious.

FYODOR MIKHAYLOVICH DOSTOYEVSKY

▣ Life is a mystery and it is beautiful because it can't be explained. The deeper we probe hidden mystical beauties, the more layers we uncover. Yet sooner or later, we will have to accept that there is a divine force at work which we cannot put our arms around.

▣ Don't try to understand or explain everything.

YOUR GRACE NOTES:

▣ ....
....
....
....
....
....

I expect the gift of good and industrious hours....
RAINER MARIA RILKE

A job is what we do for money;
work is what we do for love.
MARYSARAH QUINN

※ I produce my best work in the Summer because
the light illuminates my mind and spirit. What
work do you intend to do this Summer?

※ Work is what we do for ourselves. When we do
work we love, we are usually alone. Think about
this and what it means to you. Whatever you
create will be beautiful because it is created out
of love.

YOUR GRACE NOTES:

※ ....
....

JULY 3

If a man hasn't discovered something
that he will die for, he isn't fit to live.

MARTIN LUTHER KING, JR.

■ When you put your force and energy behind
something, the results will be powerful.

■ What are you willing to die for? Once you know,
then you can really live.

YOUR GRACE NOTES:

■ ....
....
....
....
....
....
....
....
....

♪·♪

.*T*he best thoughts most often come in the morning
after waking, while still in bed or while walking.

LEO TOLSTOY

▣   Be attentive to your thoughts first thing in the
morning before the day deals you the petty
frustrations that distract you from your best self.

▣   I've never taken a walk that was a waste of time.
It's a great time to clear one's head. Concentrate on
walking and the rest will happen spontaneously.

YOUR GRACE NOTES:

▣   ....
....
....
....
....
....
....

.... *All noble things are as difficult
as they are rare.*

SPINOZA

◾ To act magnanimously, to maintain high standards,
to be honorable, requires a commitment to
yourself. Make it.

◾ What we produce comes from who we are
spiritually. When we find ourselves in a beautiful
place inside, we can create rare, noble things.

YOUR GRACE NOTES:

◾ ....
....
....
....
....
....

*Genius, in truth, means little more
than the faculty of perceiving
in an un-habitual way.*
WILLIAM JAMES

🔲 Each fresh insight makes you see the world a little
differently.

🔲 Habits are hard to break. We become addicted to
our own ways of ritualizing our day. Change your
patterns. Drive the car to a park, or have a walk to
the train this morning. Go out in the garden to
read the mail. Shake up your day and you'll gain
new impressions.

YOUR GRACE NOTES:

🔲 ....
....

〽️🎵🎵🎵🎵🎵🎵🎵🎵🎵🎵🎵🎵🎵🎵🎵🎵🎵🎵

Grow old with me!
The best is yet to be,
The last of life,
for which the first was made.
ROBERT BROWNING

◼ Now then, after fifty we are
allowed to reflect a bit and have
some fun. Work hard when
you're young so you can reap
some rewards later.

◼ Be optimistic and keep a sense of humor. Eleanor
McMillen Brown told Peter and me that she
would die when her usefulness was up. Stay
useful, whatever your age. Think ahead so the last
of life is the dessert.

YOUR GRACE NOTES:

◼ ....
....
....
....
....

> What good mothers and fathers instinctively feel
> like doing for their babies is the best after all.
>
> BENJAMIN SPOCK

▣ Children are our treasures. Happy people are good
parents. When you love, you can follow your
instincts and you'll do fine.

▣ Don't worry. Children need to have fun with you.
Why concern yourself with rigid bath schedules?
Go have a swim together. The more creative you
are, the more fun your children will have.

YOUR GRACE NOTES:

▣ ....
   ....
   ....
   ....
   ....
   ....

In dreams begins responsibility.

WILLIAM BUTLER YEATS

🔳 We own our subconscious mind. Pay attention to
the glory as well as the nightmare because it is
your truth. When you wake up, write down your
dream. Do this every day for a month. Read your
own mind.

🔳 When something becomes clear, act on it. Trust the
process. Your intuition is speaking to you.

YOUR GRACE NOTES:

🔳 ....
....
....
....
....
....

*T*ime for a little something.

A. A. MILNE

▨ Take time to do something for a child. Send a postcard with an appropriate quotation.

▨ Have those terrific beach pictures enlarged and send one to a grandparent in an inexpensive frame.

YOUR GRACE NOTES:

▨ ....
....
....
....
....
....
....
....
....

Economy is the art of making the most of life.

GEORGE BERNARD SHAW

◼ Inner resources make us live fully and creatively with what we have.

◼ Whenever we are diminished — by bad health or financial reversals — we learn more about our character and values. While we don't seek this, we grow from it.

YOUR GRACE NOTES:

◼ ....
....
....
....
....
....

Let us, then, be up and doing...
HENRY WADSWORTH LONGFELLOW

- The more things you plan to do, the more energy you'll have. What are you going to do tonight? I'm having friends over for lobster salad.

- The picket fence could stand a coat of white paint. I love to paint, especially when I can be outside. Paint an old kitchen chair French blue. Have a child do sponge work on it in white.

YOUR GRACE NOTES:

- ....
....
....
....
....
....

I am the master of my fate;
I am the captain of my soul.

W. E. HENLEY

◼ Remember, you are in charge.
You are responsible for the
direction of your boat.

◼ Read *Care of the Soul* by Thomas
Moore, a guide for cultivating depth and
sacredness in everyday life. "No one can tell you
how to live your life. No one knows the secrets of
the heart sufficiently to tell others about them
authoritatively."

YOUR GRACE NOTES:

◼ ....
....
....
....
....
....

217

*I*t has taken me the time since you died
to discover you are as human as I am....if I am.

ROBERT LOWELL

※ Why do parents pretend to be super-human? On
my mother's deathbed she finally told me about
some of the wild urges of her youth. Tell your
children about you.

※ Children need to know that we aren't perfect and
that we too messed up as young people. Unless we
are real, our children will feel they aren't good
enough. Can you imagine a worse feeling than not
measuring up to some false standard?

YOUR GRACE NOTES:

※ ....
....
....
....

It is only when we forget all our learning
that we begin to know.

HENRY DAVID THOREAU

■ Experience life firsthand. Read a paperback copy
of *Summer* by Edith Wharton. Go outside to a
beautiful, sensuous place and sit still and read.

■ Winston Churchill and I have one thing in
common. Neither of us went to Oxford or
Cambridge. I went to art school at age sixteen,
and I don't have as much to "forget" as some of
you. Everything is still a revelation to me because
I'm ignorant of *so* much.

YOUR GRACE NOTES:

■ ....
....
....

219

*N*othing great was ever achieved
without enthusiasm.

RALPH WALDO EMERSON

▣ Enthusiasm is God within; this I learned from
reading Dr. René Dubos's *A God Within*. See if a
used bookstore can do a search for you if your
local library doesn't have a copy.

▣ What are you most enthusiastic about today? You
will have energy to burn once you pursue your
enthusiasms with passion.

YOUR GRACE NOTES:

▣ ....
....
....
....
....
....

....*All* serious daring starts from within.

EUDORA WELTY

■ Don't seek direction from others. They can't help us because they'll never know the whole picture. Listen to your gut. Once you dare, divine inspiration will be your companion.

■ Keep your passion to yourself. Let it out in your own time. Many people talk about what they're going to do but they are in denial about their inability to begin the journey. If we are serious we have to dare and just do it. Talk is cheap.

YOUR GRACE NOTES:

■ ....
....
....

I don't think there has ever been a man
who has treated a woman as an equal,
and that's all I would have asked,
for I know I'm worth as much as they.

BERTHE MORISOT

🔳 How naive I was growing up. I felt being a woman
was the greatest. I've come to realize how horribly
we have been treated over the years. I still can't
believe it. Do men really understand they wouldn't
exist were it not for women?

🔳 I do not feel superior to men, but I assure men
I do not feel inferior. I respect men and rejoice in
the difference. A self-centered superiority on the
part of either sex is obnoxious. The more loving
you are, the more understanding you'll be of
the needs of both sexes to fulfill their potential.

YOUR GRACE NOTES:

🔳 ....
....

I can forgive, but I cannot forget.

HENRY WARD BEECHER

▣ I forgive in order to move forward, but I don't forget and therefore I live accordingly. No one can make me a victim unless I allow them to.

▣ Let go of anger. It hurts you more than the person you feel rage toward. Move on. Life is too valuable to get stuck!

YOUR GRACE NOTES:

▣ ....
....
....
....
....
....
....

....*To* have taste or discernment requires a capacity
for thinking things through to the bottom....

LIN YUTANG

◾ Taste is not something we
pick up from a local store
or a decorator. First choose
a life-style that suits you and
the rest can be intelligently
thought through.

◾ How well developed is your personal style? Are
you making some changes this summer in line with
your style as you understand it today?

YOUR GRACE NOTES:

◾ ....
....
....
....
....
....
....
....

> *W*hatever is worth doing at all
> is worth doing well.
>
> LORD CHESTERFIELD

- Nothing can ever be done well unless a realistic amount of time is given to the task. When you rush, you waste time, because you will make mindless mistakes.

- What can you say no to this Summer? Cut back on your commitments if you feel pressured. It is far better to do one thing with full force than to spread yourself all around and feel fractured.

YOUR GRACE NOTES:

- ....
....
....
....
....

*M*ake haste slowly.
CAESAR AUGUSTUS

◼ Make haste slowly is the Stoddard family motto. What is yours?

◼ Peter and I changed his family motto from "Learn to die" to "Learn to love." If you have a motto, is it positive?

YOUR GRACE NOTES:

◼ ....
....
....
....
....
....
....
....
....
....
....

*C*olors are the smiles of nature....
they are her laughs, as in flowers.

LEIGH HUNT

■ Let the radiance of Summer, its colors and
warmth, bring you joy.

■ The colors that cheer you now — at the beach
and in the garden — let them become a palette for
the months ahead. Establish *your* colors and live
with them year-round.

YOUR GRACE NOTES:

■ ....
....
....
....
....
....
....
....

Come forth into the light of things,
Let nature be your teacher.
WILLIAM WORDSWORTH

■ Whenever we feel perplexed, let nature tutor us. She is available twenty-four hours a day at no expense.

■ Go out into the light. We see things more acutely in the intensity of light. Search for balance, order and beauty.

YOUR GRACE NOTES:

■ ....
....
....
....
....
....

*I was never less alone
than while by myself.*

EDWARD GIBBON

◼ Remember that all things around us are our close
friends — our books, our furniture, our bed, our
dog, our sweater, our bathrobe. My pen.

◼ Whenever I choose to be alone, a world opens up
to me. I'm able to think about those I love and
dwell on my own thoughts. How often are you
able to be alone?

YOUR GRACE NOTES:

◼ ....
....
....
....
....

The busier we are, the more acutely we feel that
we live, the more conscious we are of life.

IMMANUEL KANT

◼ We have to concentrate on our capacity to live
fully. It's not a question of expending all our
energy and feeling depleted, but of using our
energy in fulfilling ways.

◼ We gain energy by expending energy. We have
to use our lifetime as we go along. Each day
offers a wealth of opportunity for more vitality,
more heart.

YOUR GRACE NOTES:

◼ ....
....
....
....

....*To* get where you want to go,
you must keep on keeping on.

NORMAN VINCENT PEALE

- Norman Vincent Peale preached a sermon where
  he inquired, "Do you know what a big shot is?
  A big shot is a little shot that keeps on shooting."

- So often we become discouraged prematurely.
  Hang in there. Cling to what you believe is true.
  But most important, never give up your dreams.
  Keep moving your feet.

YOUR GRACE NOTES:

....
....
....
....
....
....

....*M*any small maken a great.

GEOFFREY CHAUCER

◩ It is always the accumulation of the little details, the small steps, that cumulatively make a big difference in our life.

◩ Start something today. Go for a bike ride, stop at a favorite place, and take some pictures.

YOUR GRACE NOTES:

◩ ....
....
....
....
....
....
....
....

Grace was in all her steps,
Heaven in her eye,
In every gesture dignity and love.

JOHN MILTON

■ When someone is self-assured and is able to stand tall and go about their business, they are full of grace.

■ You don't have to tell anyone your secrets but you will reveal your inner beauty in the way you carry yourself. You don't have to do anything. You are naturally beautiful whenever you are yourself.

YOUR GRACE NOTES:

■ ....
....
....

....*The* realization of the self is only possible
if one is productive, if one can give birth
to one's own potentialities.

JOHANN WOLFGANG VON GOETHE

☒ We are all extremely busy doing various jobs, but
we must make time for the work that will develop
and increase our own powers.

☒ Do you get pleasure from your work or is it just a
job? If you're unhappy, is a change realistic?

YOUR GRACE NOTES:

☒ ....
....
....
....
....
....

*W*hat we have to learn to do,
we learn by doing.

ARISTOTLE

- I love to work. I enjoy puttering. Often when I am thinking through an idea, I do something physical which fuels my writing.

- Aristotle's "active virtue" is a way to live. We do get better with practice. Concentrate on what's really important to you. Time is short.

YOUR GRACE NOTES:

- ....
....
....
....
....
....

All that we are is the result
of what we have thought.

BUDDHA

- If we think positive things, our energy will be positive. We will produce. "Think upon these things."

- A doctor recently gave a lecture stating that 85 percent of all things that people say are negative. What we think is who we are. Today, monitor everything you think and you will be in closer touch with your essence.

YOUR GRACE NOTES:

■ ....
....
....
....
....
....

The bluebird carries the sky on his back.

HENRY DAVID THOREAU

■ For a bluebird the sky is not a heavy burden. Mitzi Christian, my godmother, gave me a bluebird of happiness pin when I was little. When I was happy I wore it right side up. When I was sad, I wore it upside down.

■ When you are soaring everything is light. If you feel a weightiness about any aspect of your life today, think about the bluebird.

YOUR GRACE NOTES:

■ ....
....
....

The art of being wise
is the art of knowing what to overlook.

WILLIAM JAMES

- First things first. If you have your antennae out and are receptive to random signals you may find it is a full-time occupation, leaving you with no time for your work.

- Don't look around. Whenever you know what's important, don't seek inspiration outside of the project at hand. Apply your full energy to it.

YOUR GRACE NOTES:

- ....
....
....
....

It is through the cracks in our brains
that ecstasy creeps in.
LOGAN PEARSALL SMITH

■ Keep moving in the direction of your dreams and
you will find exaltation. What do you care about
the most? Only from focused action is ecstasy
possible.

■ What we do defines us. And the spirit with which
we do it opens us up to grace.

YOUR GRACE NOTES:

■ ....
....
....
....

A wrongdoer is often a man
who has left something undone,
not always one who has done something.

MARCUS AURELIUS

■ Whenever we don't do what we know we should,
we can kid ourselves only so long. Eventually we
have to stop blaming others for our failures.

■ Only you can put your ideas into action. August is
vacation time. Use it to develop a plan. In a few
weeks you will be on your way.

YOUR GRACE NOTES:

■ ....
....
....

AUGUST 6

The mind is slow in unlearning
what it has been long in learning.

SENECA

▦ A friend told me recently that he wished we could all start fresh and not have any ghosts from the past to haunt us.

▦ Do we wake up and suddenly see the light, or do we slowly begin to move in the direction of truth? What are you teaching your children that they will eventually have to unlearn?

YOUR GRACE NOTES:

▦ ....
....
....
....
....

*H*e only can enrich me who can recommend
to me the space between sun and sun.

RALPH WALDO EMERSON

◼ What we do from dawn to dusk is of great
significance. It's important that we don't let others
interfere with our steady resolve to live a full,
useful, productive day — while we still can.

◼ Set aside a whole day to work on a project that
will engage your full attention. To fill a day
with your energy and talent will be a powerful
experience.

YOUR GRACE NOTES:

◼ ....
....

The dream shows the inner truth and reality
....as it really is.

CARL JUNG

◪ Dreams can't be camouflaged. They are here and now and us.

◪ Mrs. Brown used to like to dream on things. I do too. If I'm in a situation I'm having difficulty resolving, I abandon it to the dream. Miraculously, it sorts itself out. Amazing grace dreams.

YOUR GRACE NOTES:

◪ ....
....
....
....
....
....
....

I have realized that the past and the future
are real illusions, that they exist only in the present,
which is what there is and all that there is.

ALAN WATTS

■ Focus on the present. You'll be less anxious.

■ Read one of Alan Watts's Zen books in paperback.

YOUR GRACE NOTES:

■ ....
....
....
....
....
....
....
....
....

*A*rt! Who comprehends her?
With whom can one consult
concerning this great goddess?

LUDWIG VAN BEETHOVEN

▨ Whenever we work on something creative, we are
solving questions. The work creates the harmony.

▨ Today, rather than seeking recognition for what
you do, do it for yourself. Let everything feed your
spirit. Inspiration is all around you. Watch for its
disguises.

YOUR GRACE NOTES:

▨ ....
....
....
....
....

You never know what is enough
unless you know what is more than enough.

WILLIAM BLAKE

🔳 Make a list of all the people and things that you could give up and still have enough. Now, nurture what's left.

🔳 How are your tomatoes this Summer? I grow basil next to my back door along with mint. What is more delicious than sliced tomatoes, basil, mozzarella and olive oil eaten in the garden with a friend? Isn't this enough?

YOUR GRACE NOTES:

🔳 ....
....
....
....

The Rainbow comes and goes,
And lovely is the Rose.
WILLIAM WORDSWORTH

■ In our village the picket fences are interlaced with great clusters of pink climbing roses in August; what a feast for the eye! Concentrate on what is right in front of you.

■ Everything is transient but the memory need not fade. And that's enough.

YOUR GRACE NOTES:

■ ....
....
....
....
....
....

Sublime — the soaring of the spirit into joy.

PETER MEGARGEE BROWN

■ "Never leave home when your garden is in bloom."
This is the advice of our friend Jack Lenor Larsen.

■ We took our vacation at
home this year and loved
the spirit of the place.
Make your home your
holiday haven.

YOUR GRACE NOTES:

■ ....
....
....
....
....
....
....
....
....
....

*Beauty as we feel it is something indescribable:
What it is or what it means can never be said.*

GEORGE SANTAYANA

■ We have an old table and Williams-Sonoma garden chairs in our backyard where I go every morning to write. I can't communicate what I experience. I can only describe the setting.

■ Not everything needs to be said. What's important is to feel and experience it.

YOUR GRACE NOTES:

■ ....
....
....
....

*S*ynergy means behavior of whole systems
unpredicted by the behavior of their parts.

BUCKMINSTER FULLER

🔲 Working together on a project can produce
amazing results when there is spirit and
collaboration.

🔲 When you are operating alone, no matter how
efficient you are, you move at your own pace.
When you work as a team that cooperates,
synergism occurs. When everything comes
together a touch of magic occurs.

YOUR GRACE NOTES:

🔲 ....
....

*G*rown-ups never understood anything for
themselves, and it is tiresome for children to be
always and forever explaining things to them.

ANTOINE DE SAINT-EXUPÉRY

■ Parents are most effective when they don't assume
the role of parent but that of trusted, caring friend,
like an older brother or sister.

■ Out of the mouths of children, wisdom is natural
because all they know is the truth as they see it.
When a child speaks, *really* listen.

YOUR GRACE NOTES:

■ ....
....
....
....
....

O world, I cannot hold thee close enough!

EDNA ST. VINCENT MILLAY

■ When we feel this way we embrace everything. We have an abundance of creative energy.

■ Meditate. Write a poem. Photograph the sunset. Paint your garden in flower. Do some creative writing.

YOUR GRACE NOTES:

■ ....
....
....
....
....
....
....
....

It's good to be just plain happy;
it's a little better to know that you're happy;
but to understand that you're happy
and to know why and how....and still be happy,
be happy in the being and the knowing,
well that is beyond happiness, that is bliss.

HENRY MILLER

▨ How often do you catch yourself and suddenly you
identify a feeling of sheer joy, rapture, bliss? How
often do you feel exhilaration? Often?

▨ Because of the telephone and the computer, we
have less memorabilia in the attic for future
generations to discover. When you feel this bliss,
write about it and leave it behind.

YOUR GRACE NOTES:

▨ ....
....
....

It is what I have done with where I have been
that should be of interest.

GEORGIA O'KEEFFE

■ Artists teach us to use the resources at hand and
create something that didn't exist before. The
result is a marriage between you and our
environment.

■ You have an interesting story to tell us. How you
tell it will express your uniqueness.

YOUR GRACE NOTES:

■ ....
....
....
....
....
....
....

There is a great probability that our loss of capacity
for enjoying the positive joys of life is largely due
to the decreased sensibility of our senses
and our lack of full use of them.

LIN YUTANG

■ Tapping into the senses doesn't cost money or take
time. By being more aware of what we are doing,
we can turn the ordinary into the extraordinary —
this brings with it exhilaration and joy.

■ Artistic expression is fundamental to a well-lived
life. Go to the art supply store with a child and buy
some poster paint, some one-inch brushes, and a
roll of white paper.

YOUR GRACE NOTES:

■ ....
....
....
....
....

*M*an....is always an individual, a unique entity,
different from everybody else. He differs by his
particular blending of character, temperament, talents,
disposition, just as he differs at his fingertips. He can
affirm his human potentialities only by realizing his
individuality. The duty to be alive is the same as
the duty to become oneself, to develop into the
individual one potentially is.

ERICH FROMM

■ We become ourselves through self-expression. The
fruits of our creativity are symbols of who we are.
Focus inward; understand that we are meant to be
very different from anyone else.

■ Establish rituals and celebrations that nurture and
honor your beliefs and desires.

YOUR GRACE NOTES:

■ ....
....

...*T*oday isn't any other day, you know.
LEWIS CARROLL

▨ Today. "To-now." Morning. Noon. Afternoon.
Evening. Moments to live and cherish. Hours of
awesome beauty. Today isn't any other day,
you know.

▨ Today is the beginning of the rest of your life.
It is a clean slate. Begin it totally refreshed and
just live it.

YOUR GRACE NOTES:

▨
....
....
....
....
....
....

*T*hink....of the world you carry within you.
RAINER MARIA RILKE

■ You feed your inner self by what you experience, what you read, what you think, who you are. Your interior world is sacred and yours alone. Guard it.

■ Reread *Letters to a Young Poet* by Rainer Maria Rilke.

YOUR GRACE NOTES:

■ ....
....
....
....
....
....
....
....

*S*tay, stay at home, my heart, and rest;
Home-keeping hearts are happiest....
To stay at home is best.

HENRY WADSWORTH LONGFELLOW

🔳 Home is a spa for the soul. Where else can we feel
this happy, where else can we putter about among
our favorite things while enjoying our family?

🔳 Home-keeping hearts are happiest. Longfellow
was right. Aren't you glad you're home?

YOUR GRACE NOTES:

🔳 ....
....
....
....
....
....

AUGUST 25

*Everything that is superfluous will flow
out of the mind, like liquid out of a full vessel.*

HORACE

🔲 Whenever I concentrate on something, the rest of
the world is temporarily less important, and the
clutter and unnecessary things don't exist.

🔲 Avoid the redundant. It slows you down. Travel
lightly in all things to maintain your vitality.

YOUR GRACE NOTES:

🔲 ....
....
....
....
....
....

How good is man's life, the mere living!
How fit to empty all the heart and the soul
and the senses forever to enjoy.

ROBERT BROWNING

■ "....if your daily life seems poor do not blame it,
blame yourself, for you are not poet enough to call
forth its riches...." Rainer Maria Rilke reminds us
to live with the consciousness of a poet.

■ We carry within us all the essentials of a happy
existence. Use the heart, soul and senses to live.
How do you define the good life? On a scale of
1 to 10, rate your life satisfactions now.

YOUR GRACE NOTES:

■ ....
....
....

That which we understand we can't blame.
JOHANN WOLFGANG VON GOETHE

■ Understanding that we can't blame anyone else for our life's disappointments is the first step toward the art of living. Take this first step and you will be free.

■ Once we stop blaming others, a whole world opens to us. Assume that everyone else is doing the best they can. *Our* task is to do *our* best, which is enough.

YOUR GRACE NOTES:

■ ....
....
....
....
....
....
....

AUGUST 28

*A*lways do right —
this will gratify some and astonish the rest.

MARK TWAIN

■ It's satisfying to do the right thing. Whenever you do you will stand tall and will feel good.

■ We always do know the difference between right and wrong. Live in the light of right.

YOUR GRACE NOTES:

■ ....
....
....
....
....
....
....
....
....

Seize the day, put no trust in the morrow!

HORACE

■ Do everything you can today. Set things in order. Begin a new project. Reach out in love. Tomorrow is a myth, a mirage. The more you push the more elusive it becomes. *You will never know tomorrow. Carpe diem. Carpe momentum.*

■ If you knew you were to die in your sleep tonight, what would you do now to satisfy your unmet needs? Live this thought and you'll always be prepared.

YOUR GRACE NOTES:

■ ....
....
....
....
....

*I*deas come from everywhere.
ALFRED HITCHCOCK

■ Nothing is unimportant. Listen for
vital clues. The cosmos is full of
ideas. Grab them from the wind.

■ Keep an open mind. When you are
receptive and open, inspiration will
flow toward you.

YOUR GRACE NOTES:

■ ....
   ....
   ....
   ....
   ....
   ....
   ....
   ....
   ....
   ....
   ....
   ....

You **can** if you think you can.

GEORGE REEVES,
Sixth Grade Teacher of Norman Vincent Peale

- ▣ Avoid telling others about your ambitions and projects. Most often they will discourage you by telling you of the problems you will encounter. Whatever you think you can produce, you can. You look able to me.

- ▣ I had an assistant who loved to say, "You can't do that." Never say never. Chip away at something monumental bit by bit. Go for it and begin September with energy and high hopes.

YOUR GRACE NOTES:

▣ ....
....
....
....
....

To burn always with this hard, gemlike flame,
to maintain this ecstasy, is success in life.

WALTER PATER

■ Once you find your path you want to stay on it
and live it fully each day. There will never be
enough time, but there will be the time you need.

■ Even though September is still warm, summer
vacation is over. Think about your work. Perhaps
you need to challenge yourself more, so you too
can burn with a gemlike flame.

YOUR GRACE NOTES:

■ ....
....
....

*G*enius is mainly an affair of energy....

MATTHEW ARNOLD

■ Ask for no greater gift from life than being in the flow, loving the work so much that you will feel as though outside of time, and in complete harmony.

■ We gain energy from being free to do those things we choose to do. We never tire when we are working on *our* projects. Energy is emotional to a large degree.

YOUR GRACE NOTES:

■ ....
....
....
....
....
....
....
....

*K*now the true value of time;
snatch, seize, and enjoy every moment of it.
No idleness, no laziness, noprocrastination;
never put off till tomorrow what you can do today.

LORD CHESTERFIELD

■ Procrastination causes depression because you
live in a state of anxiety, dread, and guilt.

■ All time is of equal value. Sunday night.
Wednesday morning. An hour is an hour
whether you waste it or use it cleverly. When
you put these moments to good use, you value
yourself and feel good.

YOUR GRACE NOTES:

■ ....
....
....
....

♪·♪

*W*ell begun is half done.

HORACE

⊠ Getting off to a good start sets the pace and spirit
of an event.

⊠ Don't wait for the ideal time to begin something
new. Now *is* the ideal time. When are you going to
begin? After you've begun and *only* after, if you
need support, call a friend you admire.

YOUR GRACE NOTES:

⊠ ....
....
....
....
....
....
....
....

The crisis of yesterday
is the joke of tomorrow.

H. G. WELLS

■ Always think about the big picture.

■ Tears turn into laughter in time.
Think about what went wrong
yesterday and how awful it was
at the time. It's disconcerting to
be the underbidder at an auction,
or to lose a client, but it isn't
worth a heart attack.

YOUR GRACE NOTES:

■ ....
....
....
....
....
....
....
....

The manner of giving
is worth more than the gift.

PIERRE CORNEILLE

■ Anything offered can be enhanced by the spirit
of the giver. Start now collecting ribbons. In the
months ahead you will be able to embellish the
most humble present.

■ Give because you want to touch someone. Put
your creative twist on every gift so the receiver
knows they have a special place in your heart.

YOUR GRACE NOTES:

■ ....
....
....
....
....
....
....

*A*ction is eloquence.

WILLIAM SHAKESPEARE

- Movement begets energy. When we act, we are richly rewarded with increased vitality.

- When our contractor installed an eighteenth-century doorframe on our cottage, people gathered and watched. Jim told us that people love to observe other people in action. Watch yourself work. You're as graceful as a dancer.

YOUR GRACE NOTES:

- ....
....
....
....
....
....

273

*Never forfeit the mystery
which is our fifth dimension.*

PETER MEGARGEE BROWN

⊞ The breadth, scope and power of life lies in the mystery, in inspiration.

⊞ The muse is alive and well in all of us and when we contemplate and ponder mysteries we get in touch with the spiritual in ourselves. That is where our strength lies.

YOUR GRACE NOTES:

⊞ ....
....
....
....
....
....

*E*verything beautiful impresses us
as sufficient to itself.

HENRY DAVID THOREAU

■ Accept the beauty offered you for what it is. Don't question it. Don't analyze it.

■ Many years ago when I was in the south of France I saw a field of red poppies that made me want to dance. We learn that we can carry these beautiful images with us wherever we are.

YOUR GRACE NOTES:

■ ....
....
....
....
....
....
....
....

The easy, gentle, and sloping path....is not the path of true virtue. It demands a rough and thorny road.

MICHEL DE MONTAIGNE

▨ If we have expectations that life will be easy, we will become frustrated and thwarted. The easy stuff doesn't teach us much. What is difficult and challenging enhances our growth.

▨ Unless something is tough it won't hold sufficient meaning to make an impression. Do what only you can do and leave the easy stuff for people who can't do what you can.

YOUR GRACE NOTES:

▨ ....
....
....

*H*e is nowhere who is everywhere.

SENECA

🔳 Make a list of your obligations. Write down
approximately how much time each responsibility
will take. Are you doing enough? Too much?

🔳 Decide what's really important and bear down on
it. Think about your time as a circle. Divide your
life like a pie. If there are too many slices they'll
become meaningless slivers and will crumble.
Better be fully engaged in something than run
around scattered.

YOUR GRACE NOTES:

🔳 ....
....
....

> *B*eware, as long as you live,
> of judging people by appearances.
>
> JEAN DE LA FONTAINE

- Be receptive; everyone's life is interesting. What's important is what happens between you and the other person.

- Why judge? The essential nature of a person is revealed through their radiance and grace.

YOUR GRACE NOTES:

- ....
....
....
....
....
....
....
....

𝒷·𝒷·𝒷·𝒷·𝒷·𝒷·𝒷·𝒷·𝒷·𝒷·𝒷·𝒷·𝒷·𝒷·𝒷·𝒷·𝒷·𝒷·𝒷·𝒷

Beauty unadorned.

APHRA BEHN

◼ This is the time of year to be a student of simplicity and see beauty in the simple.

◼ Read up on the Shakers. It helps rid us of pretension and a desire for gewgaws. Truth, beauty and light are in all things simple.

YOUR GRACE NOTES:

◼ ....
....
....
....
....
....
....
....

A sound mind in a sound body,
is a short but full description
of a happy state in this world.

JOHN LOCKE

 Whenever we are healthy, physically and
spiritually, we feel whole. When we can be at one
with our work and forget about ourselves we are
in a happy state.

 We can't always count on this wholeness but
we can aspire to it and renew our commitment
to it daily.

YOUR GRACE NOTES:

 ....
....
....
....

SEPTEMBER 15

It is a wonderful seasoning of all enjoyments
to think of those we love.

MOLIÈRE

▨ Think of your loved ones as a garden. Gather
loved ones in your mind, those living and those
dead.

▨ There is really no reason to feel lonely so long as
you love. Whom are you thinking of now?

YOUR GRACE NOTES:

▨ ....
....
....
....
....
....

*Though nothing can bring back the hour
Of splendor in the grass, of glory in the flower.*

WILLIAM WORDSWORTH

🔲 Photographs capture the moments before they fade away. Press a flower and send it to a friend.

🔲 Nature teaches us about time, about being there at the harvest.

YOUR GRACE NOTES:

🔲 ....
....
....
....
....
....
....
....

A threefold cord is not quickly broken.

ECCLESIASTES

▨ Peter and I fell in love in September. "Try to remember the day in September....follow, follow, follow."

▨ My wedding ring was the least expensive band of gold sold at Tiffany's. It cost fifty-five dollars. It's a threefold cord.

YOUR GRACE NOTES:

▨ ....
....
....
....
....

Those pleasures so lightly called physical.

COLETTE

▨ Sensual delights are available to us always.
Walking, hiking, swimming, holding hands.
Hugging. Loving. Ah.

▨ When I wrote *Living a Beautiful Life* the copy editor
couldn't believe I was suggesting *another* bubble
bath. I don't bathe to get clean as much as I bathe
to feel rejuvenated and sensual.

YOUR GRACE NOTES:

▨ ....
....
....
....
....
....
....

Paradise is where I am.

VOLTAIRE

🔲 Wherever you are right now has the potential to be paradise. You are in the center of your universe because this happens to be where you are and that is of utmost importance. Where are you?

🔲 When is the last time you experienced euphoria? It's all about harmony and grace.

YOUR GRACE NOTES:

🔲 ....
....
....
....
....
....
....

...We never listen when we are eager to speak.

DUC DE LA ROCHEFOUCAULD

- Listening requires catching the words and thoughts in an attentive, generous way. Silence can be a way of demonstrating love.

- Practice listening today.

YOUR GRACE NOTES:

- ....
....
....
....
....
....
....
....
....
....

Be ye lamps unto yourselves.
Be your own reliance.
Hold to the truth within yourselves
as to the only lamp.

BUDDHA

☒ When we are independent and able to tend to
our own needs — spiritual, intellectual, physical,
emotional and material — we are free to love
each other fully. Being self-sufficient is rare
and beautiful.

☒ The truth makes us free. Illuminate yourself and
you will have the opportunity of lighting candles in
dark corners for others too.

YOUR GRACE NOTES:

☒ ....
....
....

I had been my whole life a bell....

ANNIE DILLARD

■ A bell is a still life until you shake it. The ringing of bells gives us hope. They are symbolic of both joy and alarm. Bells get us going. Ring a bell.

■ I've hung some crystal bells from the handle of the front door, and every time someone comes or goes there's a little jingle that spreads joy.

YOUR GRACE NOTES:

■ ....
....
....
....
....
....
....

*Guided by my heritage of a love of beauty
and respect for strength — in search of
my mother's garden, I found my own.*

ALICE WALKER

☒ We all search for someone else's garden until we
discover we have to plant our own and nurture it
ourselves.

☒ A friend told me I'm tough. I accept it as a
compliment. You can be strong and also caring. Be
proud of your strength and nurture it.

YOUR GRACE NOTES:

☒ ....
....
....
....

*W*hile you are upon earth,
enjoy the good things that are here.

JOHN SELDEN

◼ Don't save anything good for later. Good is always
timely. When we enjoy goodness we are living in
grace. An abundance of good is good!

◼ What good things are you experiencing today?
Make a list; make it long.

YOUR GRACE NOTES:

◼ ....
....
....
....
....
....

If you can keep your head when all about you
Are losing theirs and blaming it on you....
Yours is the Earth and everything that's in it.

RUDYARD KIPLING

▣ Don't get upset just because everyone else is. You
know what's real and what's false. Remain calm
and breathe deeply.

▣ No one else can blame you and make you
wrong unless you accept the accusation and feel
guilty. It's human nature to blame someone else;
otherwise we would have to face ourselves. Others
can complain, criticize and admonish you, but you
are free to disagree and feel innocent.

YOUR GRACE NOTES:

▣ ....
....
....

*Nature never deceives us;
it is always we who deceive ourselves.*

JEAN-JACQUES ROUSSEAU

■ I don't have a lot of fun or do very well when I
am not true to myself. Everything becomes
burdensome. Remind yourself today of what's
important to you. Be very clear with yourself.

■ The trees are changing. So are we. We're not
the same persons we were a year ago. What
tangible differences do you see in yourself? Do
you accept them?

YOUR GRACE NOTES:

■ ....
....
....

....*K*eep growing quietly and seriously
throughout your whole development.

RAINER MARIA RILKE

◨ Great accomplishments are the result of a
well-lived, well-defined life. The deeper your
growth the less sure you will be about anything.
That's a sure sign of maturity.

◨ Everyone grows at different times in different
ways. John Bowen Coburn believes we live in
chapters. What new period are you bringing to
light and what doors are you closing? You can't
add in depth without giving up some surface.

YOUR GRACE NOTES:

◨ ....
....
....

The great mind knows the power of gentleness.
ROBERT BROWNING

Look not thou down but up!
ROBERT BROWNING

▣ In the twenty-eight years of seeing Eleanor Brown
regularly I never saw her lose her gentleness. She
didn't have to because she was full of grace.

▣ I had an art teacher who admonished us to look up
and some of us have found a world of difference
because of her advice.

YOUR GRACE NOTES:

▣ ....
....
....
....
....

Follow your bliss.

JOSEPH CAMPBELL

■ Bliss is inside us and we have to live it, believe
in it and experience it so our life will be a song.

■ Sing it. Love it. Become it. On our deathbeds,
let's have a chat and see how we did. The time for
living is right now. Live at ten while you can. Time
diminishes our options, but fight it.

YOUR GRACE NOTES:

■ ....
....
....
....
....
....

*H*itch your wagon to a star.

RALPH WALDO EMERSON

■ No thought is too big or wonderful for tonight.
Explode with joy and make your life worthwhile.

■ September had it all. Temperature, scenery and
love. Carry it with you into the activities of
October.

YOUR GRACE NOTES:

■ ....
....
....
....
....
....
....

You're searching, Joe, for things that don't exist; I mean beginnings. Ends and beginnings — there are no such things. There are only middles.

— ROBERT FROST

FALL

While I thought that I was learning how to live, I have been learning how to die.

LEONARDO DA VINCI

Grace does not pressure — but offers.

— JOHN BOWEN COBURN

Live as if you were to die tomorrow.
ISIDORE OF SEVILLE

⊠ Everyone says this but too few people feel the intense urgency of time. Peter does. In serenity he steps up the pace to knowledge, understanding and love.

⊠ There are lots of important things to focus on. Don't get bogged down with chores. Consider turning everything into a grace note. Live in this state of grace and be ready to die tomorrow.

YOUR GRACE NOTES:

⊠ ....
....
....
....
....
....
....

The teeming autumn,
big with rich increase.

WILLIAM SHAKESPEARE

▣ Wherever we live, October calls us to New
England to walk in the woods and have a picnic
on a mountaintop.

▣ The dying is part of the renewal and the colors are
calling out to us to live. Hurry on and live.

YOUR GRACE NOTES:

▣ ....
....
....
....
....
....
....

*C*ease to ask what the morrow will bring forth,
and set down as gain each day that Fortune grants.

HORACE

■ Some of us live to be thirty. Some of us make it to
sixty. There are those who make it to one hundred.
Imagine the mystery in all of this fortune.

■ What you do today may have a profound effect on
your life tomorrow, if you have a life tomorrow.
Do it all now and relax.

YOUR GRACE NOTES:

■ ....
....
....
....
....
....

*H*ope is the thing with feathers
That perches in the soul,
And sings the tune without the words,
And never stops at all.

EMILY DICKINSON

- We can't hope we won't die. Paying too much
  attention to death is a waste of time because it is
  gaining on all of us. Our job is to celebrate the
  light of day and be grateful.

- Hope for feathers in your soul. Be uncomplaining
  and focus on feathers.

YOUR GRACE NOTES:

- ....
  ....
  ....
  ....
  ....

The contented mind is the only riches,
the only quietness, the only happiness.

GEORGE PETTIE

- To feel satisfied is a grace note. Be of good cheer
as you reconcile yourself to enjoying your
existence and making something significant of it.

- A quiet, pleased mind absorbs beauty and grace
naturally. Relax; be calm and be content.

YOUR GRACE NOTES:

....
....
....
....
....
....

*W*here there is sunshine the doctor starves.

FLEMISH PROVERB

■ Spend as much time outside as you can now because dark wet gloomy days are ahead.

■ We are dependent on sunshine. If it is rainy and dark, light a candle and turn on a halogen lamp and create the illusion of sunlight.

YOUR GRACE NOTES:

■ ....
....
....
....
....
....

*O*ne world at a time.

HENRY DAVID THOREAU

🔳 Peter called his last book of essays *One World at a Time*; these were the last words of Henry David Thoreau. What will your last words be? Something to ponder in the crispness of the season.

🔳 When we do a good job in whatever challenges there are, we are *living*. Tackle each thing you do with a keen sense of joy. Chopping wood, for example.

YOUR GRACE NOTES:

🔳 ....
....
....

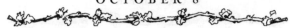

This is the mark of a really admirable man:
steadfastness in the face of trouble.

LUDWIG VAN BEETHOVEN

■ When things are going well, we aren't called upon
to be brave. But when we face really difficult
times, it is a comforting feeling to know we have
the necessary muscle to cope.

■ Whenever you face a hardship, feel anxious,
nervous and sad, embrace your pain and agony.
Know that you can learn from your misery and
pain and share the knowledge with others.

YOUR GRACE NOTES:

■ ....
....
....

308

That it will never come again
Is what makes life so sweet.
EMILY DICKINSON

⊠ We should live life with all our might now and let the rest take care of itself. Our job is to live *this* life. Concern with another life at the expense of this one diminishes our precious time.

⊠ The fact that every moment is unrepeatable and sacred is in our hands now.

YOUR GRACE NOTES:

⊠

....
....
....
....
....
....

....*The* nature of all life is to
preserve and affirm its own existence.
ERICH FROMM

▦ Are the people you surround yourself with
affirming and confirming? We don't need anyone
to remind us how difficult and tough life is. We
need encouragement to face each day.

▦ We have to instill dignity and reverence in
everyday life. What is more important than to
make something of ourselves?

YOUR GRACE NOTES:

▦ ....
....
....

Jump.

JOSEPH CAMPBELL

⊠ To jump takes maximum willpower and resolve. Better to jump than to be mousy.

⊠ Choose what's really important because you will run out of time. It's better to live with gusto than to be afraid and watch life pass you by.

YOUR GRACE NOTES:

⊠ ....
....
....
....
....
....
....
....
....
....

To look up is Joy.

CONFUCIUS

🔲 The bright side is the light side. Look up. Remain optimistic, and you will experience joy.

🔲 Whenever we look up our spirits are lifted along with our body. To look up is Joy.

YOUR GRACE NOTES:

🔲
....
....
....
....
....
....
....

*W*ith malice toward none,
with charity for all,
with firmness in the right,
as God gives us to see the right.

ABRAHAM LINCOLN

*I*t is not who is right that counts
but to be right.

ROSE MARIE MORSE

▣ Go about your life doing what you believe is right
and hold fast to your beliefs.

▣ Appreciate all the help you can get along the way,
as you try to stay on course. How are you doing on
your journey? How do you feel right now?

YOUR GRACE NOTES:

▣ ....
....
....

*A*ll is for the best in
the best of all possible worlds.

VOLTAIRE

※ We don't have a choice about where we land on
earth but we can make the best of what we have.
If we don't, we diminish ourselves.

※ Make the best of your situation. Be brave. We all
have to be to survive.

YOUR GRACE NOTES:

※ ....
....
....
....
....
....

*B*elieving where we cannot prove.

ALFRED, LORD TENNYSON

🔳 Have faith in yourself and in your family and friends. Have faith in the world. It's innocent until proven guilty.

🔳 Mystery adds excitement to ordinary happenings. Have faith in the process.

YOUR GRACE NOTES:

🔳 ....
....
....
....
....
....
....

*M*en seldom give pleasure
where they are not pleased themselves.

SAMUEL JOHNSON

■ We give in proportion to what we have. We can't give something we don't own.

■ If you go to a museum exhibit that excites you, send a postcard to a friend and spread your enthusiasm.

YOUR GRACE NOTES:

■ ....
....
....
....
....
....
....
....

$\mathcal{W}$hen I am working on a problem, I never
think about beauty. I think only of how to solve the
problem. But when I have finished, if the solution is
not beautiful, I know it is wrong.

BUCKMINSTER FULLER

⊠ Beauty is the hidden dimension inside every
problem we have to solve. Whenever we become
fascinated by anything that isn't beautiful, we too
will discover it is wrong.

⊠ What problems are you trying to solve? Write
them down. Jot down some notes about them. Let
your mind work out beautiful solutions. Puzzles
can be full of intrigue and beauty.

YOUR GRACE NOTES:

⊠ ....
....
....

317

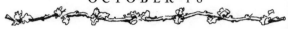

*A*las, I have done nothing this day! What? Have you not lived? It is not only the fundamental but the noblest of your occupations.

MICHEL DE MONTAIGNE

The times when we don't work, when we simply soak in the day, when we break away from the pressure and stress, bring release, refreshment and renewal.

Take a break. Give yourself a day off.

YOUR GRACE NOTES:

....
....
....
....
....
....

*L*earn to wish that everything should come to pass
exactly as it does.

EPICTETUS

▣ Who wrote the script? Do everything you can to
bring good fortune your way but then let go.
Ultimately, what is, is, and you can thrive in this
reality.

▣ Do you believe everything happens for the best?
I don't. Some things that happen to us are horrible
and very painful. But look even at that reality as a
friend and teacher.

YOUR GRACE NOTES:

▣ ....
....
....

It is a very great thing to think as you like;
but, after all, an important question remains:
what you think.

MATTHEW ARNOLD

☒ We are all free to think what we like, but we have
to think noble thoughts if we intend to accomplish
true, honorable deeds. Think high.

☒ Think healthy, positive thoughts. Go for a walk
and concentrate on where your mind wanders. If
you have a few dark spots, examine them. It is
thought that provokes action, so be careful with
your thoughts.

YOUR GRACE NOTES:

☒ ....
....
....

OCTOBER 21

*W*oman must not depend upon the protection of man,
but must be taught to protect herself.

SUSAN BROWNELL ANTHONY

Once we are adults we should seek to protect
ourselves and not live under the wing of a
provider.

If you were alone in this world and had to support
yourself, what would you do to earn a living?
What skills do you have? What experience? Think
about providing for yourself.

YOUR GRACE NOTES:

....
....
....
....
....
....

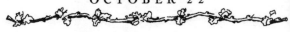

To me every hour of the light
and dark is a miracle....
WALT WHITMAN

🔲 Live each hour of light with depth, concentration
and focus. Welcome darkness for dreams and rest.

🔲 Each hour of light offers the possibility — the
miracle — of seeing something for the first time.
Experience this in people, places, and things.

YOUR GRACE NOTES:

🔲 ....
....
....
....
....
....

322

Philosophy is perfectly right in saying that life must
be understood backward. But one forgets the other
clause — that it must be lived forward.

SØREN KIERKEGAARD

■ It helps me to live life fully when I think about
the inevitability of death. It's
not about how old we are
but about how much time
we have left to be productive.
You realize quickly that you're already on
fast forward.

■ What do you want to have accomplished by next
October? What can you do today to put the
wheels in motion? Think about it as you rake
leaves.

YOUR GRACE NOTES:

■ ....
....
....
....
....

The best way out is always through.
ROBERT FROST

▣ When you are faced with a difficult time you can get through it better by focusing on what you hope to accomplish. Be strong, do what you have to do, and move forward.

▣ Facing reality isn't always easy. But it is wise to look at the problem objectively, intelligently, and then act. Problems don't get better on their own. Sooner is better when you need to figure something out.

YOUR GRACE NOTES:

▣ ....
....
....

I do the very best I know how,
the very best I can.

ABRAHAM LINCOLN

▨ We shouldn't be so hard on ourselves that we stop trying. Wherever we are we can do our best and that's all that will ever be expected of us.

▨ Your best is good enough. As the holiday season builds in momentum, we should make plans that are good for ourselves as well as for our family and friends. No one will have false expectations unless you allow it. We never let others down without first letting ourselves down. Do the very best you can and relax.

YOUR GRACE NOTES:

▨ ....
....
....

The ideals which have always shone before me
and filled me with the joy of living
are goodness, beauty and truth.

ALBERT EINSTEIN

■ Even if you are blessed with superior intelligence,
there is only so much time in life to form and live
worthwhile ideals. Think about yours and what
fills your life with joy.

■ Take your camera with you and go on a bike ride
and photograph the colors of the trees. One road
near our cottage forms natural arches of oak, elm
and maple. This sight fills me with goodness,
beauty and truth.

YOUR GRACE NOTES:

■ ....
....
....
....

There are those who bring something to this life which others can only observe. Me? God gave it to me because I was lucky. *And I never let it go.*

RUDOLF NUREYEV

☒ What are your God-given gifts? Don't ever let them go. When we have talent we are blessed.

☒ We become good at something when we have a natural bent and we follow it with hard work. What were you good at as a child that you've given up as an adult? Piano? Singing? Painting? Dance?

YOUR GRACE NOTES:

☒ ....
....
....
....
....

A generous action is its own reward.

WILLIAM WALSH

- We make a generous, spirited, sincere gesture because it is rewarding and brings us satisfactions.

- The pleasure is always in the process. What are you doing for someone that makes you feel good?

YOUR GRACE NOTES:

....
....
....
....
....
....
....
....
....

*L*ife rushes from within....
WILLA CATHER

■ The richer our imagination, the richer our life. Do you like to daydream?

■ Translate the creation of your imagination into reality. You may be one of the blessed who has more ideas than time. Keep the surplus in a journal, to be tapped into later for inspiration.

YOUR GRACE NOTES:

■ ....
....
....
....
....
....

A letter always seemed to me
like Immortality.

EMILY DICKINSON

▣ The advantage of the telephone is that it lets us
hear someone's voice, but it leaves nothing for
history or posterity. Pick up your pen, not the
telephone, and write your son at college.

▣ A note on a postcard can be savored and remain
on someone's desk for months. Stack a collection
of postcards on your desk and start using them to
send grace notes to friends — a joke or a thought
for the day.

YOUR GRACE NOTES:

▣ ....
....
....

*All I care about is life, struggle, intensity.
I am at ease in my generation.*
ÉMILE ZOLA

- I don't like Halloween and never did. Do you feel silly in costumes? But nevertheless, have a Halloween party so your children and their friends will be safe within your home.

- If you don't have young children at home, this is a night like any other. Be productive and make a contribution to your generation.

YOUR GRACE NOTES:

- ....
....
....
....
....
....
....

331

*M*an lives in the world but once.

JOHANN WOLFGANG VON GOETHE

▨ We're all given a chance, but only one — to make something of our lives.

▨ I love November. Halloween is behind us and we celebrate Thanksgiving. Each day is a lifetime. Live it close up, in detail. Think about your world and your life and what you want to be remembered for when your time is up.

YOUR GRACE NOTES:

▨ ....
....
....
....
....
....
....

"I have done my best." That is about all
the philosophy of living that one needs.

LIN YUTANG

◼ Isn't it interesting that many of the great thinkers
from all over the world say pretty much the same
things? The best way to do our best is to work on
improving ourselves.

◼ Doing your best is the only philosophy you will
ever need, but you must follow through with
action. Remember, doing your best will be easier
if you are on the right track.

YOUR GRACE NOTES:

◼ ....
....
....
....

*A*ny profound view of the world is mysticism.

ALBERT SCHWEITZER

- ⊠ Love the questions. The bigger the questions, the better. The mysteries of life have never been understood by any human so far and never will be.

- ⊠ The little things that make you happy, the order you put into your corner of the universe, the joy you feel from these small rituals, are mysterious. You're not crazy; you're creative. It's all right if you are teased. Who cares? You do these things for yourself.

YOUR GRACE NOTES:

- ⊠ ....
....
....
....

There is no need to run outside for better seeing ...
Rather abide at the center of your being;
for the more you leave it the less you learn.
Search your heart and see....The way to do is to be.

LAO-TZU

▨ Running around doesn't help you remain centered.
"The way to do is to be" is one of those quotations
that is worth repeating. Think about it today. *Do*
less. *Be* more.

▨ Learn to see by allowing for unstructured time.
Free yourself to think things through without
pressure and deadlines. Whenever I search my
heart, I do see. Have some good seeing time today.

YOUR GRACE NOTES:

▨ ....
....
....

*L*ife is real! Life is earnest!

HENRY WADSWORTH LONGFELLOW

■ I've been thinking about why great people are so remarkable. Isn't it because they enlarge our vision? These people we admire remind us of the abundant possibilities waiting for us.

■ We can make a sincere effort to make our lives rich. A happy, productive person teaches us about happiness and productivity. We can make a difference in our world when we believe in our capacity to live abundantly. What's real in your life? Live it.

YOUR GRACE NOTES:

■ ....
....
....

*I*t is better to suffer wrong than to do it,
and happier to be sometimes cheated than not to trust.

SAMUEL JOHNSON

⊠   I've been cheated. Have you? I try to surround
myself with trustworthy people and I put my trust
in them.

⊠   There are some human beings to whom I would
entrust my future and on whom I would bet my
life. Think about trust — whom *you* put your trust
in and who trusts *you*. Trust is earned.

YOUR GRACE NOTES:

⊠   ....
....
....
....
....
....

NOVEMBER 7

The superior man makes the difficulty
to be overcome his first interest;
success comes only later.

CONFUCIUS

- We read biographies to learn about the struggles
  and hurdles that men and women overcame
  in their courageous and dauntless efforts to
  accomplish their goals.

- Everyone has difficulties to resolve. Life is not for
  the fainthearted, the pusillanimous complainer.
  Expect great challenges and face them head-on.
  This is the way to go and success comes from
  surviving heroically.

YOUR GRACE NOTES:

- ....
  ....
  ....

𝒯he secret of success is consistency of purpose.
BENJAMIN DISRAELI

▨ First, evaluate and reevaluate your goals. Then
have a plan, a design, so your efforts will add up to
achieve the desired results.

▨ I was born on November 8. I enjoy birthdays as
markings to reflect on my consistency of purpose.
We do need consistency — no matter how
numerous and varied our objectives are.

YOUR GRACE NOTES:

▨ ....
....
....
....
....

...*W*hen you are required to exhibit strength,
it comes.

JOSEPH CAMPBELL

■ We're given a surge of power when necessary.
You'll discover muscle you never knew you had.
Reach out to friends, mentors and spiritual
leaders. You don't need to be alone.

■ Energy and vigor increase as you need it. We
never know how much endurance we have until
we are tested.

YOUR GRACE NOTES:

■ ....
....
....
....
....

*W*hat a man thinks of himself....
determines, or rather, indicates his fate.
HENRY DAVID THOREAU

■ Try never to think negative thoughts about
yourself. They can't help and they will hurt you.
You are largely what you think you are.
Value yourself.

■ Self-confidence increases with accomplishments.
What are some of the things you've done that you
are proud of and that you consider worthwhile?
What are your plans now? Often we feel better
about ourselves after we've made a list of our past
achievements.

YOUR GRACE NOTES:

■ ....
....
....

The word is half his that speaks
and half his that hears it.
MICHEL DE MONTAIGNE

▨ Keeping the essential balance between speaking
and listening is key to improving ourselves and
achieving greater depth. Try not to talk unless you
have to. Talk to yourself a lot and try to hear more
of what others have to say.

▨ When we speak about something it is difficult to
write about it also. We write what we think we
haven't already said. Is this why writers have to be
alone so much?

YOUR GRACE NOTES:

▨ ....
....
....
....
....

We know of no culture that has said, articulately,
that there is no difference between men and women
except in the way they contribute to the creation
of the next generation.

MARGARET MEAD

 Men and women are one. We have the same
yearnings, the same longings. We aren't that
different in the soul. By being aware of this we
can help and encourage one another to live the
opposite side of our human nature.

 I once remarked to a friend that I live a man's life
and was told, "No, you live a full life." Think of the
things you want to do to broaden your life by
giving up gender-based roles.

YOUR GRACE NOTES:

 ....
....
....

*M*arriage, to women as to men, must be a luxury,
not a necessity; an incident of life, not all of it.

SUSAN BROWNELL ANTHONY

◪ My own marriage is a full partnership. Peter and I
mutually contribute to each other and together we
take care of each other. It's a luxury waking up
beside each other every day.

◪ Is your marriage a luxury? I never think about the
marriage contract; I think about our mutual love,
support and companionship. Think about your
marriage today.

YOUR GRACE NOTES:

◪ ....
....
....

*O*ur personal journeys mark us.
DAVID HALBERSTAM

■ Get personal. What do you really care about?
What you spend your time doing becomes your
chosen life-style.

■ Whether we're married or not, our journey is
individual. We don't have joint obituaries. We
can love others but we cannot live our own life
through the lives of others.

YOUR GRACE NOTES:

■
....
....
....
....
....
....

*W*hat you do not want others to do to you,
do not do to others.

CONFUCIUS

⊠ I try to live by the Golden Rule. When people
treat me badly I try to be understanding. Their
behavior most likely stems from anger and
frustration.

⊠ What are the things that others do that are most
irritating to you? Do you ever do things to others
you would hate them to do to you? Make up your
mind today that you won't judge others who have
a different perspective from your own.

YOUR GRACE NOTES:

⊠ ....
....
....

*L*et us not overstrain our talents,
for if we do we shall do nothing with grace....

JEAN DE LA FONTAINE

■ Everyone wants to pull his own weight but don't
push beyond your limit. You don't need to be
miserable in order to do your best work. Often
the best comes pouring out when you are in a state
of grace.

■ How many people are coming for Thanksgiving
dinner? Make it a giving feast where everyone
brings something and you will feel in touch with
the founding men and women of America.
Gather family and friends together and share in
the banquet.

YOUR GRACE NOTES:

■ ....
....
....

*C*heerfulness keeps up a kind of daylight in the mind,
and fills it with a steady and perpetual serenity.
JOSEPH ADDISON

🔳 Try to be cheerful. When we appear cheerful
it is because we are experiencing a kind of
daylight. If we program our minds with optimistic,
hopeful thoughts, we will be happier, moment by
moment. Train your mind to be in a good mood.

🔳 We have different personalities, temperaments and
natures. How would you describe your character
and disposition? Have you always been this way?
Do you believe you can change your nature? I do.
We can choose our attitude toward life, and then
live it.

YOUR GRACE NOTES:

🔳 ....
....
....

*W*hen kindness has left people,
even for a few moments, we become afraid of them,
as if their reason had left them.

WILLA CATHER

  We can always tell when someone has lost their
goodwill toward us because they no longer act
graciously, sympathetically and lovingly. People
don't actually have to say or do anything to be
offensive. When they no longer show compassion,
watch out.

  Your life is not a popularity contest. There will be
people who won't like you, as hard as that is to
believe. If someone is cruel and mean toward you,
avoid them.

YOUR GRACE NOTES:

  ....
....
....

*D*esire nothing for yourself
which you do not desire for others.

SPINOZA

⊠ Our grace and joy do not take away from others.
Instead, they will bring hope to others.

⊠ As a former tennis player I realized that only *one*
person could win the tournament. But playing well
makes everyone live up to their own potential.

YOUR GRACE NOTES:

⊠
....
....
....
....
....
....
....
....

The sage is one who has first discovered
what is common in our hearts.

MENCIUS

■ We feel we are alone in our strivings but we are
not. Pain makes us reach out, and when we do we
connect and realize that others, too, have traveled
along the same path. This is how we grow.

■ I wrote *Living a Beautiful Life* for myself, as a way
of clarifying the importance of the rituals we
create in our daily life. Over the years I've learned
that these little things matter greatly to our spirit
and mood. We're connected.

YOUR GRACE NOTES:

■ ....
....
....

*L*abor to keep alive in your breast
that spark of celestial fire called conscience.

GEORGE WASHINGTON

🔲 Be careful in *all* you think and do, because when
you are honest, you will be of good conscience.

🔲 Be particular and you will be
meticulous in all your transactions.
The flame of the celestial fire is
sparked by being precise today.

YOUR GRACE NOTES:

🔲
....
....
....
....
....
....
....
....
....
....

*W*hoever cultivates the golden mean avoids both
the poverty of a hovel and the envy of a palace.

HORACE

※ This Thanksgiving season focus on the true
meaning of giving thanks and showing
appreciation. We all want to live a good life. We
can thank those who have helped us and we can
reach out to others in need.

※ Someone could benefit from a pot of homemade
soup. In the spirit of the season, rather than
donating canned goods or a check, make some
soup and donate it to your church or temple.
People will line up in appreciation.

YOUR GRACE NOTES:

※ ....
....
....

Time is a sort of river of passing events.
MARCUS AURELIUS

▣ Candles symbolize passages. Thanksgiving, Hanukkah, Christmas. Prayers, celebrations and rituals. Gather together a selection of colored candles that will carry you through the season — have a variety of sizes and shapes, including short beeswax ones, and light them.

▣ What's not important is the perfect meal. Let go of unrealistic expectations. There's always awkwardness with celebrations that bring together the extended (often untraditional) family. Enjoy as much of the ceremony as you can.

YOUR GRACE NOTES:

▣ ....
....
....

*...A*s we get deeper, we move closer and closer to other people; we feel closer to life as a whole.

EKNATH EASWARAN

■ I must have been a choirboy in a cathedral in another life. I love to light candles and look at the flame and reflect. Do you? I feel connected when I light candles and think about spiritual things.

■ It's all about connecting. Sharing ourselves with others. Each Thanksgiving there have been different people at the table. It's also a time to celebrate those who are no longer able to join us.

YOUR GRACE NOTES:

■ ....
....
....
....
....

*C*hange everything, except your loves.

VOLTAIRE

■ The world seems in chaos. We are forced to go along with radical changes in the hope they are for the common good. But we never have to change our loves.

■ When love is genuine it grows. As we approach the most stressful time of the year, when everyone is expected to feel love, be lovable and joyful, remember those loved ones who are essential to your life.

YOUR GRACE NOTES:

■ ....
....
....
....
....

*H*umanity will find in itself the power
to live for virtue even without believing
in immortality. It will find it in love
for freedom, for equality, for fraternity.

FYODOR MIKHAYLOVICH DOSTOYEVSKY

- Not everyone believes in deathlessness. But we
  should all believe in eternal truth, light and
  the dignity of man. Freedom should entail
  responsibility for fraternity, if not love.

- Faith is beautiful if it helps you to live a beautiful
  life, and be kind and loving to yourself and others.
  If you find you are leaning on your faith the way
  you would a pair of crutches, remember that God
  helps those who help themselves.

YOUR GRACE NOTES:

- ....
  ....
  ....

Surprised by joy.

C. S. LEWIS

🔲 When is the last time a friend made you laugh to tears? Share a funny story with someone. Tell a joke.

🔲 I love the stuffing more than the turkey. A friend brought me some stuffing for our feast this year. While enjoying the corn stuffing I think of him. Every gift is an excuse to think of a loved one and to feel joy.

YOUR GRACE NOTES:

🔲 ....
....
....
....
....
....

𝒥 believe....that every human mind
feels pleasure in doing good to another.

THOMAS JEFFERSON

🔳 Take pleasure in reaching out and giving to others.
Think of someone who is really needy and doesn't
expect something from you. And surprise them.

🔳 Be sure your ribbon box has lots of pretty colors,
designs and textures so you're ready to deck the
halls and tie bows on little gifts.

YOUR GRACE NOTES:

🔳 ....
....
....
....
....
....
....

*Z*en is a way of liberation, concerned not
with discovering what is good or bad
or advantageous, but what is.

ALAN WATTS

  For most people, this season is the most stressful,
anxious time of the year. Be kind to yourself.
Accept the way you feel. It's all right.

  As you begin the frantic pace, remember there are
three hundred and sixty-five days in the year. You
can't do everything at the end. Simplify.

YOUR GRACE NOTES:

  ....
....
....
....
....
....

*T*he sun shines to-day also.

*T*here are days when the great are near us,
when there is no frown on their brow....There are days
which are the carnivals of the year.

RALPH WALDO EMERSON

- Have a friend over for tea. Serve cinnamon melba toast and have a *real* talk. This time of year when the pressure to spend money is intense, calm down and give the most precious gift. Give of yourself.

- Remember Emerson's advice: "In stripping time of its illusions, in seeking to find what is at the heart of the day, we come to the quality of the moment...."

YOUR GRACE NOTES:

- ....
....
....

Think to yourself that every day is your last;
the hour to which you do not look forward
will come as a welcome surprise.

HORACE

⊠ There is no need to become stressed out, nervous
or sad when the pace quickens. You can't give
away more than you have. Take extra care of
yourself so your immune system doesn't become
depleted.

⊠ Live each day, each hour, in harmony with
who you are and what your life represents. It's
worthwhile to try.

YOUR GRACE NOTES:

⊠ ....
....
....
....
....

....*A*ppreciate the present hour....
Sit and hear your own breathing and look out
on the universe and be content....One does not
have to do something to pass the time;
time can pass by itself.

LIN YUTANG

■ Our breathing is indicative of how we feel and
how we are handling stress. Take lots of deep
breaths and relax. Nothing is worth health
problems.

■ How do you feel right now? Are you appreciating
the present hour? Make some lemon tea and use a
cinnamon stick to play with the lemon slices and
enjoy a few moments of peace. Put on some of
your favorite holiday music.

YOUR GRACE NOTES:

■ ....
....
....

*C*ontentment consisteth not in adding more fuel,
but in taking away some fire.

THOMAS FULLER

■ In the past, this time of year, we've
had a tendency to overdo. Too
many obligations, too many
parties, too many deadlines that
dull our senses. Enjoy a steady
flame but not a continual bonfire.

■ Every invitation doesn't require your presence.
Consider spending some quiet evenings at home
with your feet up, relaxing by the fire — not
socializing and not working, just living.

YOUR GRACE NOTES:

■
....
....
....
....
....
....
....
....

It is not of so much consequence what you say,
as how you say it.
ALEXANDRA SMITH

▣   This is the time of year when we exaggerate our
demands. Be extra-cautious to be kind and
courteous to all those people who seem frazzled
and short-tempered. It's no time for a shouting
match.

▣   Tone of voice sets off vibrations. The way your
face looks, the way you gesture — for example,
aggressively pointing your finger — can hurt
someone's feelings. Everything is revealing.
Be careful.

YOUR GRACE NOTES:

▣   ....
....
....

Strong is the soul, and wise, and beautiful....
MATTHEW ARNOLD

※ Your spirit, your essence, is at the heart of everything about you. The way you act is a reflection of the core of your being.

※ No one can disturb your center unless you allow them to. Has anyone upset you lately? Don't let their angst interfere with your grace. You are not in control of them, but you are in control of yourself.

YOUR GRACE NOTES:

※ ....
....
....
....
....
....
....

*H*umanistic ethics may very well postulate happiness
and joy as its chief virtues, but in doing so it does not
demand the easiest but the most difficult task of man,
the full development of his productiveness.

ERICH FROMM

❋ We don't need to be told what to do. We know.
With freedom comes the responsibility to take the
difficult path and go the extra mile. What efforts
are you making to be fruitful?

❋ What are you doing for New Year's Eve? Do you
feel like staying at home and having a romantic
evening for two? Or do you want to have a few
close friends over for a dinner party? Decide and
make plans. Either way, you can't lose.

YOUR GRACE NOTES:

❋ ....
....
....

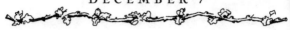

A man's style is as much a part of him as his face,
his figure, or the rhythm of his pulse.

FRANÇOIS FÉNELON

▣ Our style becomes more flamboyant this season
when we festoon everything with garlands,
ornaments and ribbons. Our home will reflect our
exuberance for life and the holiday spirit.

▣ We develop a personal style that really does mirror
our soul. If we pick up a style that is not our own,
we will pay dearly by being a stranger in our own
house. Carry on in your own way with your own
loving traditions and your style will be refreshing.

YOUR GRACE NOTES:

▣ ....
....
....

> *To* live well is to work well,
> to show a good activity.
> THOMAS AQUINAS

■ We are all quite pleased with ourselves when we've accomplished something. Forced idleness is enervating. Don't give all your time to visits and group activities if this means neglecting your own work.

■ Privately set mini goals for yourself and work on them every day. In time you will make good progress. Eat dinner early so you have two or three hours to work before bedtime. Resist telling yourself you're tired and watching television.

YOUR GRACE NOTES:

■ ....
....
....

*W*hat wound did ever heal but by degrees?

WILLIAM SHAKESPEARE

■ Not all family members get along. You can't force things. If you feel the pain of a recent loss, don't expect the healing to be immediate. Light a candle and think about those you love; give in to a bit of sadness. It's natural.

■ Each new year we replace pages in our loose-leaf daybook where we've lost a loved one or a friendship has faded. Life goes on and you will have a deeper capacity to love and empathize in the coming year.

YOUR GRACE NOTES:

■ ....
....
....

*I*magination is more important than knowledge.
ALBERT EINSTEIN

■ When we imagine, we wonder and hope and invent. We can't nail everything down concretely. Your creativity and inspiration are yours alone and can't be learned in a textbook.

■ What are some visions you have for the days ahead? What fantasies do you cherish? Dare to dream big dreams because from my experience they come true.

YOUR GRACE NOTES:

■ ....
....
....
....
....

*W*hy, sometimes I've believed as many as
six impossible things before breakfast.

LEWIS CARROLL

■ One of the most endearing qualities about
someone is their playfulness. Dream the impossible
dream. Dare the impossible act and, after
breakfast, make it all come alive.

■ When I have a lot to do I find it calms me to make
a list. Call them grace notes — things to do, people
to see, places to go. It's amazing how much more
we can accomplish by ordering our priorities and
beginning.

YOUR GRACE NOTES:

■ ....
....
....
....
....

*P*unctuality is the politeness of kings.

LOUIS XVIII

■ Resolve to allow a lot of time to get to places.
There is more traffic now and you need the extra
minutes to stay calm. It's pleasant to have a few
grace moments at a restaurant before you meet
a friend.

■ Being early sends loving signals that you are
looking forward to the visit. A friend came to
see us and was early so he went for a walk and
watched the new moon.

YOUR GRACE NOTES:

■ ....
....
....
....
....
....

*N*othing to excess.

INSCRIPTION IN THE
TEMPLE OF APOLLO AT DELPHI

☒ I have four peach tulips on my working desk. Just
enough to remind me of Spring and let me reflect
on flowers. I think that flowers are a metaphor for
our living beautifully and they remind us that
nothing lasts.

☒ I always regret it whenever I overdo anything.
Overwork, overeat, overdrink, overanalyze,
overwrite. Remember the Indian doctor who told
my aunt, Ruth Elizabeth Johns, "Moderation in
everything, Betty, even virtue." Be moderate and
let go.

YOUR GRACE NOTES:

☒ ....
....
....

No man who is in a hurry is quite civilized.

WILL DURANT

🔳 We've had all year to plan and arrange for the holidays. Rushing around makes you crazy and everyone around you nervous. Don't speed up your pace. Get in the flow. Participate in the celebration of everything joyfully.

🔳 I hate to rush anything. Do you enjoy wrapping packages? I love selecting pretty boxes, lining them with coordinated colorful tissue and tying a ribbon around them, then making sassy bows. I also like to put many of the trinkets I give to friends in decorative shopping bags. The box, the ribbon and the bag can be reused.

YOUR GRACE NOTES:

🔳 ....
....
....

*T*he wise man will want to be ever with him
who is better than himself.

PLATO

▦ Invite someone you admire to
have lunch with you. This is the
time of year when we are starved
for some real conversation and a
few generous hours of undivided attention.

▦ One of the reasons we feel empty after going to a
crowded, noisy, catered cocktail party is that we
haven't touched anyone or been touched. Better
spend an hour in a corner with one person than
chitchat the night away.

YOUR GRACE NOTES:

▦ ....
....
....
....
....
....
....
....
....

*W*hen you are content to be simply yourself and
don't compare or compete, everybody will respect you.

LAO-TZU

■ What a good message for now. Someone will give
you an elaborate gift and you haven't given that
person so much as a card. Be yourself and be a
generous, loving recipient.

■ It is not the spirit of the season or the message to
think tit for tat. On Christmas evening last year we
received a phone call that so-and-so hadn't gotten
anything from us. You can't please everyone.
It's okay.

YOUR GRACE NOTES:

■ ....
....
....

The things which hurt, instruct.
BENJAMIN FRANKLIN

▨ What are some of the things that have hurt your feelings? Disappointment, loss, misguided expectations, dishonesty, misrepresentations — every experience in life teaches us. In fact, we are tutored individually. Learn to be your own counselor and instruct yourself when you hurt.

▨ What have you learned this past year that has changed you and made you deeper and wiser?

YOUR GRACE NOTES:

▨ ....
....
....
....
....

We cannot get grace from gadgets.

J. B. PRIESTLEY

◾ Our fax is a good, modern machine, but it is temperamental. We rely on this machine. When it gets jammed our nerves become jangled because we can't see our way out. How many gadgets we acquire and how frustrating they become!

◾ Gadgets, remember, are great when they work. Grace isn't something you acquire by calling the repairman. Try to rely less on gadgets and feel grace.

YOUR GRACE NOTES:

◾ ....
....
....
....
....
....

*N*ever hating, never resisting, never contesting,
she is simply always learning and being.

LAO-TZU

🔲 Open yourself up to learning and being. Is your
house decorated? We used ribbons as our theme
this year, putting bows on our wreath and tree.
What is the theme of your decorations?

🔲 What have you learned from your friends and
neighbors about their traditions and religious
observations? Embrace all influences and rituals
and celebrate love and joy together.

YOUR GRACE NOTES:

🔲 ....
....
....
....
....

*L*ess is more.

LUDWIG MIES VAN DER ROHE
(Borrowed from Robert Browning)

Last year everyone wanted to just get through the holidays so life could get back to normal. Don't put any extra pressures on yourself. Keep things simple so you can live in the spirit of the season.

This is a month of potential excess. Avoid overload which leaves you feeling dull. Give your spouse a present early — a book you know will be a hit, perhaps. Stay home by the tree and read.

YOUR GRACE NOTES:

....
....
....
....
....
....

Time is the least thing we have....
ERNEST HEMINGWAY

▦ When we don't have enough time we put our life on fast-forward. I enjoy spending time with family. We can see friends the rest of the year.

▦ Get your responsibilities behind you — all your deadlines —so you can indulge yourself enjoying your home. Once it gets this close to Christmas I like my work to be wrapped up until the new year. This should be a time for you.

YOUR GRACE NOTES:

▦
....
....
....
....
....

*It is only with the heart that one can see rightly;
what is essential is invisible to the eye.*

ANTOINE DE SAINT-EXUPÉRY

▣ See with your heart. The really important things
aren't tangible, like happiness, which is very
elusive. There's a lot of tinsel this time of year.
Love can be sprinkled around all the other
months too.

▣ What do you see? Is there a whole lot of love in
the air? I feel it. Last Christmas was the first
one we spent in our new cottage in Connecticut.
The house is now christened and feels warm
and cozy.

YOUR GRACE NOTES:

▣ ....
....
....

I love those who yearn for the impossible.

JOHANN WOLFGANG VON GOETHE

🔳 We enlarge ourselves by imagining the unthinkable. This is a marvelous time of year, when we have symbols and celebrations, music and candles to bring us together in love.

🔳 Don't listen to anyone who tells you what you can't do. Only you know what you yearn for. Don't be afraid of anything. Miracles, mysteries, myths and memories merge.

YOUR GRACE NOTES:

🔳 ....
....
....
....
....
....

I did not wish to live what was not life,
living is so dear; nor did I wish to practice resignation,
unless it was quite necessary. I wanted to live deep and
suck out all the marrow of life....if it were sublime,
to know it by experience...

*B*e it life or death, we crave only reality.

HENRY DAVID THOREAU

▨ The effort we put into these cere-
monies around the table, holding
hands, the tenderness we express
toward each other is all we need
to know about reality and love.

▨ We create our own reality by the way we ritualize
life. I want to live deep and suck out all the
marrow of life....I know it is sublime. I'm
living it.

YOUR GRACE NOTES:

▨ ....
....
....

*R*ing out, wild bells, to the wild sky!

I cannot understand; I love.
ALFRED, LORD TENNYSON

■ Merry Christmas! And may you feel a great deal of joy. After all the intense preparations, we can all relax at home. There's black bean soup on the stove. Dinner tonight by candlelight and the fire at eight.

■ This is the year for practical presents — Alexandra and Brooke gave me a blue and green plaid bathrobe I will live in. The real gifts were being together, lingering over the dining table talking and throwing log after log after log onto the fire.

YOUR GRACE NOTES:

■ ....
....
....

386

I knew very well what I was undertaking, and very
well how to do it, and have done it very well.

SAMUEL JOHNSON

■ We all made it through the holidays. This is a
bathrobe day. Cozy, comfortable and relaxed. All
our efforts have paid off as usual. Alexandra and
Brooke took brisk walks, wrote thank-you notes
and planned their New Year's Eve party.

■ You should be proud of yourself for all you have
accomplished. Think of all those people you
reached out to in loving ways. I love seeing the
happy mess all over the house, the wrinkled white
linen napkins, the dirty wine glasses and the
crumbs from last night's banquet.

YOUR GRACE·NOTES:

■ ....
....
....

The aim, if reached or not, makes great the life;
Try to be Shakespeare, leave the rest to fate.
ROBERT BROWNING

▨ Whenever we aim high, we live with greater intensity and satisfactions. Our fortune is flexible; the
higher our sights, the better our fate.

▨ What are your thoughts for the new year?
What are your new goals? Did you know that
Shakespeare used approximately fifty-four
thousand different words? Try to be Shakespeare.
It will improve your vocabulary and make life
more interesting.

YOUR GRACE NOTES:

▨   ....
    ....
    ....
    ....
    ....

DECEMBER 28

*H*ow many cares one loses when one decides not to
be something but to be someone.

COCO CHANEL

🖾 Everything falls into place as soon as we find our
personal style. Being comfortable with ourselves is
an accomplishment.

🖾 Who do you know who is pure and true to their
unique spirit? As we think about the new year, let's
plan lots of space for reflection and time for the
work we love. It's worth whatever sacrifices are
necessary.

YOUR GRACE NOTES:

🖾 ....
....
....

*T*here's only one corner of the universe
you can be certain of improving
and that's your own self.
ALDOUS HUXLEY

- A doctor told me that no human being can ever
  change another more than approximately five
  percent. And even then, the person can have
  relapses. We can, however, improve ourselves.

- Write down a few things you want to work on to
  improve yourself this coming year. Begin by
  resolving to use your energy in positive,
  constructive, life-enhancing, optimistic ways.

YOUR GRACE NOTES:

- ....
  ....
  ....

I regret nothing.
EDITH PIAF

- I've learned a great deal this year. I feel it has been productive and also enjoyable day to day. What a wonderful thought to live our lives with as few regrets as possible.

- What kind of a year did you have? How would you rate it? No matter how many challenges you've had, no matter what pain you've endured, did you do your very best? Then have no regrets.

YOUR GRACE NOTES:

....
....
....
....
....
....
....

> ....*B*ut all shall be well, and all shall be well,
> and all manner of things shall be well.
>
> DAME JULIAN OF NORWICH

▨ I hate endings. I wish you a vital, happy, healthy
New Year. Fill the moment and tomorrow with
many grace notes and love. When you do, joy will
follow.

▨ We're all connected. Twenty years ago Peter gave
me a hand-hammered gold necklace made up of
interconnected links. To us it symbolizes *our*
interconnectedness. This is not an ending but a
beginning of notes between us — and more grace.

YOUR GRACE NOTES:

▨ ....
....
....

ACKNOWLEDGMENT
WITH APPRECIATION

Carl Brandt
Thank you for being my literary adviser and
trusted friend since I wrote my first book outline.
True, I write to please myself, but when *you* are
satisfied, my joy doubles. I appreciate your belief
in me, your wisdom, caring and *you*.

Peter Megargee Brown
I've loved all our reading over these past two
decades. Thank you for your insights, your advice,
and our wonderful conversations. You make the
quest an exciting process. Your contributions to
my thinking, my work, and my life are invaluable.
I love you.

Alexandra Brandon Stoddard
I love you. What a joy to live grace notes with you
wherever we may be.

Brooke Goodwin Stoddard
I love you. Your enthusiasm, your smile, and your
French connection continue to spread grace.

Rose Marie Morse
Thank you for enthusiastically jumping in to
become my new editor. You didn't skip a beat,
making the transition stimulating. I admire
your intelligence, vision, inspiration, and
commitment. Thank you for the depth you bring
to the work.

Marysarah Quinn
You embody the message that work is what you
love most to do. Working with you is play. Don't
ever lose your divine inspiration. Thanks, Babe.
Each book design is more exciting than the last,
and full of grace.

Stephen Freeburg
Where have you been all my life? Your eye, your design sensibility, your touch, and your artistic talent help express freshness, spirit, and grace.

Skip Dye
Thank you for coming up with the idea of a whole book of fresh, new, daily grace notes.

Bob Aulicino
I enjoy working with you on my book jackets, all the way back to the work you did on the cover of *Living a Beautiful Life*, where my grace notes were introduced.

Sarah Zimmerman
Thanks for being at our right hand.

Patsy Corbin
Thanks for pointing the way to Steve, and for always suggesting grace to me.

Elisabeth Carey Lewis
I appreciate all your grace, daily assistance and love.

John Bowen Coburn
Thank you for being a "Grace Bearer" to me. Our friendship spreads joy and "Grace upon Grace."

My Readers
You are the inspiration behind this book. Thank you for letting me know how much Grace Notes make a difference in your lives, and for sharing yours with me in your beautiful letters.

Alexandra Stoddard

Stonington Village

INDEX

397

MORE GRACE NOTES:

....
....
....
....
....

....
....
....
....
....

....
....
....
....
....

....
....